MAXIMISE YOUR MARK

food technology
revision guide

JULIE BOOKER
BARBARA MONKS
HELEN ROBERTS
JULIE STAFFORD

SERIES EDITOR: TRISTRAM SHEPARD

Text © Tristram Shepard and Nelson Thornes Ltd 2003, 2004
Original illustrations © Nelson Thornes Ltd 2003

The right of Julie Booker, Barbara Monks, Helen Roberts, Julie Stafford to be identified as authors of this work has been asserted by them in accordance with the Copyright, Designs and Patents Act 1988.

All rights reserved. No part of this publication may be reproduced or transmitted in any form or by any means, electronic or mechanical, including photocopy, recording or any information storage and retrieval system, without permission in writing from the publisher or under licence from the Copyright Licensing Agency Limited, of 90 Tottenham Court Road, London W1T 4LP.

Copy by any other means or for any other purpose is strictly prohibited without prior written consent from the copyright holders. Application for such permission should be addressed to the publishers.

Any person who commits any unauthorised act in relation to this publication may be liable to criminal prosecution and civil claims for damages.

Published in 2004 by:
Nelson Thornes Ltd
Delta Place
27 Bath Road
CHELTENHAM
GL53 7TH
United Kingdom

05 06 07 08 / 10 9 8 7 6 5 4 3 2

A catalogue record for this book is available from the British Library

ISBN 0 7487 8995 2

Illustrations by Tristram Ariss and Tristram Shepard
Page make-up by Turchini Design, London
Picture research by Sue Sharp

Printed and bound in Croatia by Zrinski

Acknowledgements
Special thanks are due to Sheena Yull for her detailed comments and suggestions.

The publishers are grateful to the following for permission to reproduce photographs and other illustrative material:

Anthony Blake Photo Library (p 38 middle, p 56 right, p 58 top)
Art Directors & TRIP Photo Library (p 15 top, p 22 right, p 30 bottom right, p 33 middle, p 34 bottom right, p 37, p 48 top right, p 50 top, p 56 left, p 57 middle right)
British Meat Education Service (p 31 bottom, p 49 middle)
Canterbury Foods (p 32 top and middle)
Chilled Food Association (p 58 middle left)
Corel Corporation (p 18 lower middle and bottom, p 20 right, p 24 right, p 35 top right, middle centre and right, p 54 middle, p 58 bottom)
Hemera Technologies Inc. (p 4, p 5 top and bottom, p 6, p 8, p 15 middle right, p 16, p 17, p 18 middle, p 20 middle, p 23 right, p 24 bottom, p 25 top right and bottom left, p 26 bottom left, middle and right, p 27 top right, p 28 top right, p 29, p 30 left, p 32 bottom right, p 33 bottom, p 35 middle, p 36 middle and bottom, p 39 top and middle, p 42 lower middle and bottom, p 45 middle, p 47 top right, bottom and middle left, p 53 middle right, bottom left, middle and bottom right, p 57 top right and middle left)
Instant Art (p 58 bottom)
James Holmes / Farmer Giles Foods (p 28 left)
Martyn F Chillmaid (p 7, p 9, p 15 left, p 19 middle and bottom, p 24 left, p 38 bottom, p 39 bottom, p 40, p 41, p 42 top and middle centre, p 46, p 47 middle, p 48 top left, middle and bottom left, p 49 bottom right, p 50 middle and left, p 51 top, p 52 middle and bottom, p 53 top and top middle, p 55 top right and middle left, p 56 left, p 61)
MORI (p 27 middle)
Quark Inc. (p 44 top)
Sainsbury's (p 21 middle right, p 22 left, p 27 left, p 30 top, p 35 top middle, p 57 middle right)
Science Photo Library/Bernhard Edmaier (p 21 top)/Andrew McClenaghan (p 49)/Ed Young/AGSTOCK (p 63), Science Photo Library (p 38 middle, p 59)
Tesco (p 27 left)

Every effort has been made to contact copyright holders. The publishers apologise to anyone whose rights have been inadvertently overlooked and will be happy to rectify any errors or omissions.

Contents

Introduction	4
Improve Your Technique	5
Revision Planning Charts	10
Study Guide Topic 1 **Food** Materials and Components (1)	15
Study Guide Topic 2 **Food** Materials and Components (2)	20
Study Guide Topic 3 Industrial Food Product Design (1)	25
Study Guide Topic 4 Industrial Food Product Design (2)	30
Study Guide Topic 5 Food Production Systems	35
Study Guide Topic 6 Packaging and Labelling	40
Study Guide Topic 7 Social and Economic Implications	46
Study Guide Topic 8 Combining Ingredients	51
Study Guide Topic 9 Mechanical and Industrial Equipment	56
Study Guide Topic 10 Industrial Food Safety	59

Introduction

Maximise Your Mark has been developed to help make revision for the GCSE written paper more worthwhile, and more enjoyable. It provides a comprehensive, structured programme of study and revision that helps you identify what you know and don't know. The first section also gives you tips on the best ways to tackle questions.

There are a number of ways in which you might use this book:

- as a weekly programme of study during the final year of your GCSE course
- as a revision checklist to work through in the months just before you take the written paper.

The book is divided up into ten topics that cover the examination specification. Most topics have five sections, but some have three, four or six. Each section is contained on a single page and includes an example question for you to try. Each section also includes a handy cross-reference to pages in the GCSE *Design & Make It! Food Technology* textbook, where you will find a more details. Keywords and relevant web-links are provided, where appropriate.

A CD-Rom version of this book may be available in your school. Ask your teacher if it is on your school's network, or on any stand-alone PCs, and if there are copies of the CDs you can purchase for home use. The electronic version also includes animated illustrations, multiple-choice questions, sample answers with examiners' comments and a full glossary.

The Design & Make It! team hope that *Maximise Your Mark: Food Technology Revision Guide* will make an important and effective contribution to your success in the written paper.

Good luck in your exams!

Tristram Shepard
Series editor

Maximise Your Mark Food Technology

Improve Your Technique

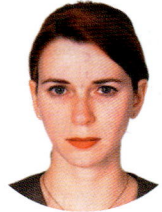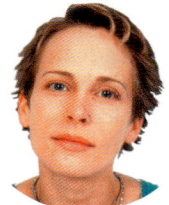

Did you know that doing well in your Design & Technology written paper involves more than just knowing all the information contained in this study guide? You also need to know how to tackle the particular types of questions you will be asked – what the examiner is going to be looking for, how long to spend on each answer, how to use examples to support your answer, etc.

The study and revision techniques you are learning in your other subjects are going to be very useful with D&T too, but the D&T written papers are a little bit different from most of the others that you sit. The next few pages are intended to help focus your revision on exactly what's required for the Food Technology examination.

Top Tips

Here are five top tips to help you maximise your mark:

1. Read the question very carefully
2. Look closely at the available marks for each part of the question
3. Use the marks as a guide to how long you should spend on each question
4. Use Food Technology keywords and phrases whenever possible
5. Remember to use your coursework

1 Read the question very carefully

Sounds obvious doesn't it? However, many students throw marks away simply because they've not paused for a moment and checked what's really being asked for. It's all to easy to spot a couple of familiar words in a question and start writing everything you know about them. No D&T question ever works like this!

Each question is asking you to reveal and apply your knowledge in some way. For example, you may need to:

- discuss the advantages and disadvantages of...
- provide a number of examples of...
- explain what is meant by a specific term when used in a particular situation...

Maximise Your Mark Food Technology

- Advantages and disadvantages
- Analyse
- Calculate
- Compare (and contrast)
- Describe
- Detail
- Develop
- Differences (and similarities)
- Draw
- Evaluate
- Give reasons
- Identify
- Label
- List
- Name
- Outline
- State
- Study
- Using notes and sketches

On the left are some other words commonly used in questions – you need to be clear on what each is instructing you to do.

When the examiner comes to mark your paper he or she has to follow a set mark scheme that matches the specific requirements of each question. So if there are two marks for giving two advantages and two marks for giving two disadvantages, you can only score a maximum of half-marks if you only discuss the advantages – however many you cover. In a similar way, you'll lose marks if you fail to provide the correct number of examples required.

2 Look closely at the available marks for each part of the question

To make life a bit easier, the D&T written papers give you plenty of information about how many marks are available for each part of each question. In some cases it might even show you that there are, say, two marks for stating the advantages and two for the disadvantages. In another it might be a little less obvious, but it's usually quite easy to work out what the marking scheme is going to be. For example, what do you think the marking scheme for the following question is likely to be?

> When designing new food products the developers need to be aware of the functions of each ingredient during the manufacturing process. For example, the main ingredients of flaky pastry are flour, fat, salt and water. Explain the function of each of these ingredients *(12 marks)*

Here's one student's answer to this question:

> The flour is the main ingredient and gives bulk to the mix. Strong plain flour is used because it has more gluten, which makes the dough more elastic.
> The fat used is margarine, which gives a good flavour and colour and produces the layers when it is added between the folds of dough. It gives a good crisp texture.
> Salt improves the flavour. Water holds the mixture together.

And here's an explanation by an examiner of where the student gained and lost marks:

> This student would have gained eight out of twelve for this answer. He has carefully explained the function of each ingredient, and gained a mark for each correct point. He then earned further marks where he has provided a fuller explanation.

> However, the student left out some important additional facts. Look closely where the student scored and lost his marks:

- The flour is the main ingredient and gives bulk to the mix. *(1 mark)*
- Strong plain flour is used because it has more gluten which makes the dough more elastic *(2 marks)*.

Maximise Your Mark Food Technology

- The fat used is margarine *(1 mark – a second mark is lost here for not mentioning the use of lard).*
- which gives a good flavour and colour *(1 mark).*
- and produces the layers when it is added between the folds of dough. It gives a good crisp texture. *(1 mark – a second mark is lost here for not saying which of these is the lard's function.)*
- Salt improves the flavour. *(1 mark. More detail would have given an extra mark.)*
- Water holds the mixture together. *(1 mark. One final lost mark for not stating that the water changes to steam during cooking and this helps the pastry to rise.)*

A question like this is challenging. It involves more than simple factual recall as it tests your understanding. As always, it's important to read the question and check the mark allocation to ensure you are making enough points in each part of your answer.

It's important to get into the habit of providing detailed examples and explanations. Unless the question asks for a list, it's unlikely that a simple one word answer is going to be enough to get you the marks. Basically for each section you study or revise you can pre-prepare a number of examples or explanations, and then use whichever supports the answer to the question most effectively.

During your course you should get to know the names of some food products and manufacturers. Try to use specific examples in which you provide the full product name and manufacturer. So instead of just saying 'a low-fat healthy option fish product' you could use an example like 'Sainsbury's cod fillets in parsley sauce ready meal, from their "Be good to yourself" range, which claim to contain less than 5% fat'. Make sure the marks available are worth the trouble of a specific example like this.

Here's another question:

> Compare the reasons a food manufacturer might consider for using chilling or cook-chilling rather than freezing for processing some food products. Make particular reference to the needs of the consumer. *(10 marks)*

Here is one student's answer:

> If food products are frozen then they need to be thawed and this can take a long time. People need to have a freezer to store frozen foods.
>
> Cook-chilled foods are ready to reheat. Chilled fresh foods taste nice and look good. Consumers can see they are fresh.
>
> Most people want food quickly and so cook-chill products suit them.

Maximise Your Mark Food Technology

This student scored 6 marks for her answer. So where did she lose the other 4 marks? Here's what an examiner explained:

> More marks would have been awarded if this student had included more specific detail, for example:
>
> – Frozen foods need to be stored at −18°C to −29°C, so therefore consumers need to have a freezer to store them for longer than 24 hours.
>
> This student needs to aim to use specific adjectives or descriptive phrases. For example, 'look appetising' is better than just 'look good', and 'Have an authentic fresh flavour' is a considerable improvement on 'tastes nice'.
>
> To maximise her mark, this student needs to think around the topic and include a wider range of points. A mention of the fact that some foods do not freeze very well could have been made, or that there is a wider range of products available chilled or cook-chill than in the frozen range. She might also have referred to the fact that freezing is a more severe treatment and may cause damage to parts of the products.

Although this student didn't get the maximum mark, it's always worth trying to answer questions even if you can only put down a few points. You might run out of time, or just not be able to think of the right answer for all parts of the question. The first few points you do make may get you some reasonably good marks towards the final grade.

3 Use the marks as a guide to how long you should spend on each question

In the D&T written papers there's a very simple guide as to how long to spend on each question – a mark a minute! So if a question is worth six marks you should be spending around five or six minutes attempting to answer it. If it only takes you, say, one minute, then perhaps you've not provided enough detail? If the six minutes is nearly up and you're only halfway through, then you're probably writing far too much.

Remember that you'll need to include some initial time to read the question and think about your answer – don't just start writing. Start by checking the mark scheme, working out what examples you are going to use, thinking of the appropriate technical terms, etc.

With D&T papers you are advised to attempt the answer the questions in the order in which they are set. This is because the answer to one may lead on to the answer to a previous question. However, it's still important not to spend too much time on a question you are finding difficult. Do what you can in the given time, and then move on. If there's time left at the end you can then go back and try to finish it off.

Maximise Your Mark Food Technology

4 Use Food Technology keywords and phrases whenever possible

On each page of the study guide that follow you'll find a number of keywords. You need to know what each one means and how to use it correctly in a sentence. You will find that you already know what many of them mean, which is just as well as in all there are about two hundred! Whenever you come across a word or phrase you are not familiar with, make a point of finding out what it means – ask your teacher or look it up in a textbook. If your school has the *Maximise Your Mark: Food Technology* CD-Rom you can check the glossary, or use the QuickSearch option.

Aim to use as many of these keyword terms as possible in your written paper: they really help show that you know what you're talking about. In many questions each one you use might easily earn you an extra mark, and make the difference between one grade and another.

It's also a good idea to try and remember the group of keywords that apply to each section. When you come across a question that relates to that section, thinking of as many keywords as possible will help you recall quickly recall a much wider range of information, and you might also be able to use some of the other keywords in your answer.

5 Remember to use your coursework

Sometimes questions ask you to refer to your GCSE coursework, perhaps as an example. Be aware that the person marking your written paper will not have seen your practical work or design folder, so you will probably need to give some brief information about what you designed and made.

You may find it helpful to think back to your coursework. For example, if you need to give an example of something designed for batch production, the work you did during your course might help remind you of the key points.

Other questions might show you a photograph of a product and ask you to develop its specification, or undertake an analysis and evaluation of it. You will have probably done similar exercises during your course. Although the product might be slightly different, think back to the sort of observations you made, and see if they apply to this example.

Finally, remember that the examination attempts to find out what you *do* know and understand, not what you don't. We all hope you manage to Maximise Your Marks!

MAXIMISE YOUR MARK

Revision Planner

Name: _____ Form: _____

Food Technology

Topic 1 Food Materials and Components (1)	Topic / Section Start Date	Target Finish Date	Actual Finish Date	End of Topic Review ✓ How well did I do on the written paper question? How could I have maximised my marks?	End of Topic Review ✓ What do I need to revise again for this section?
Section 1 Commercial methods of creating food components and materials					
Section 2 The composition, structure and properties of proteins, fats, starches and sugars					
Section 3 Manipulating food materials and components to create a desired effect					
Section 4 Ratios and proportions					
Section 5 Alternative ingredients					

Topic 2 Food Materials and Components (2)				End of Topic Review ✓	
Section 1 The addition of heat					
Section 2 The removal of heat					
Section 3 Controlling temperature					
Section 4 Acids, alkalis and micro-organisms					
Section 5 Smart materials					

MAXIMISE YOUR MARK

Revision Planner

Name: _____ Form: _____

Food Technology

	Topic / Section Start Date	Target Finish Date	Actual Finish Date	End of Topic Review ✓
Topic 3 — Industrial Food Product Design (1)				How well did I do on the written paper question? / How could I have maximised my marks? / What do I need to revise again for this section?
Section 1 The changing needs of target groups				
Section 2 Investigating customer views				
Section 3 Gathering information from a range of sources				
Section 4 Design specification and product formulation				
Section 5 Prototypes				
Topic 4 — Industrial Food Product Design (2)				End of Topic Review ✓
Section 1 Testing prototypes				
Section 2 Manufacturing specification				
Section 3 Standard components				
Section 4 Quality control				
Section 5 HACCP				

11

MAXIMISE YOUR MARK

Revision Planner

Name _____   **Form** _____

Food Technology

Topic 5 Food Production Systems	Start Date	Target Finish Date	Actual Finish Date	How well did I do on the written paper question? How could I have maximised my marks?	What do I need to revise again for this section?
Section 1 Production process systems					
Section 2 CAD: manufacturing simulations					
Section 3 Computer Aided Manufacture (CAM)					
Section 4 Sensors and control					
Section 5 Critical points in controlled testing				End of Topic Review ✓	

Topic 6 Packaging and Labelling					
Section 1 Why is food packaged?					
Section 2 Packaging materials					
Section 3 Packaging requirements					
Section 4 Food labelling					
Section 5 Using CAD in packaging					
Section 6 Nutritional information on packaging				End of Topic Review ✓	

MAXIMISE YOUR MARK

Food Technology — Revision Planner

Name: _____ Form: _____

Topic / Section	Start Date	Target Finish Date	Actual Finish Date	End of Topic Review ✓	How well did I do on the written paper question? How could I have maximised my marks?	What do I need to revise again for this section?
Topic 7 — Social and Economic Implications						
Section 1 Social, moral, cultural, economic and environmental issues						
Section 2 Healthy eating						
Section 3 Genetically modified and organic foods						
Section 4 Additives – good or bad?						
Section 5 Packaging and the environment						
Topic 8 — Combining Ingredients				End of Topic Review ✓		
Section 1 Recipe development						
Section 2 Solutions and suspensions						
Section 3 Combining ingredients and processes						
Section 4 Designated tolerances						
Section 5 Why are additives used?						

MAXIMISE YOUR MARK

Revision Planner

Name: _____ Form: _____

Food Technology

Topic 9 — Mechanical and Industrial Equipment

- **Section 1** Processing equipment
- **Section 2** Consistency of outcome
- **Section 3** Computer controlled processes

Topic 10 — Industrial Food Safety

- **Section 1** Micro-organisms and enzymes
- **Section 2** Food contamination and spoilage
- **Section 3** Risk assessment
- **Section 4** Safety and hygiene rules
- **Section 5** Storage of food commodities

Topic / Section	Start Date	Target Finish Date	Actual Finish Date	End of Topic Review ✓	How well did I do on the written paper question? How could I have maximised my marks?	What do I need to revise again for this section?

14

Topic 1 Study Guide 1 — Food Materials and Components (1)

Here's what you need to know...

about commercial methods of creating food components and materials.

See *Design & Make It! Food Technology* Revised pages 108, 111, 130, 132–133 (22–23 earlier edition).

KEYWORDS
Do you know what the following terms mean?
- Primary processing
- Secondary processing
- Pasteurised
- Milled
- Refined
- Hydrogenation
- Sieved
- Raising agents

WWW.
Go to:
www.foodtech.org.uk

The Food Technology Industry

Making a meal at home is not the same as manufacturing a food product to be sold in a supermarket. The processes of production involved are very different. You need to have a good understanding of how food products are developed and manufactured in industry for the written paper.

Why is Food Processed?

Most food materials require some sort of processing before they can be sold in a supermarket. There are two main ways of classifying the processing of food materials: **primary processing** and **secondary processing**.

Primary processing
This involves working with a raw food material to make it either ready for eating, or ready to be used as a suitable ingredient for secondary processing. For example:

- Milk is always **pasteurised** to make it safe.
- Wheat is **milled** into flour.
- Eggs are sorted for size, as are many fruits such as bananas, melons and peppers.
- Seeds may be **refined** into oils, such as sunflower oil.
- Nuts and fruits may have oils extracted from them – like olive oil, for example.
- Soya beans are **fermented** to create soy sauce.

Secondary processing
This is further change to the food material in order to make some other useful food product. For example:

- Soft fruits are made into jam.
- Milk is processed to become yoghurt or cheese, it is sterilised or canned as evaporated milk or condensed milk.
- Flour is made into self-raising flour or bread.

Processing methods
There are many methods of processing food, both at the primary and secondary levels. Heat is used for most commercial processing, like canning, **cook-chill** and UHT. Removal of heat also helps processing by freezing and chilling.

To make margarine, first the sunflower oil needs to be extracted from the seed. To remove any impurities the oil is then refined. Finally, it is put through a **hydrogenation** process to convert it to a spreadable margarine.

Written Question

Spend about 9 minutes answering the following question. You will need some paper and something to write with.

Explain briefly how:

a) Sunflower oil is made into margarine. *(3 marks)*
b) Milk is made safe by pasteurising. *(3 marks)*
c) Wheat becomes self-raising flour. *(3 marks)*

Milk is pasteurised to destroy any harmful bacteria. It is heated to 72°C for 15 seconds and then quickly cooled to below 10°C.

To make self-raising flour the wheat grain has to be milled. The white flour is then **sieved** with precisely measured **raising agents**.

Topic 1 Study Guide 2 — Food Materials and Components (1)

Here's what you need to know...

about the composition, structure and properties of proteins, fats, starches and sugars.

See *Design & Make It! Food Technology* Revised pages 34–35, 72 (26, 64 earlier edition).

KEYWORDS
Do you know what the following terms mean?
- Protein
- Biological value
- Fats
- Sugars
- Starches

www.
Go to:
www.nutrition.org.uk

Proteins

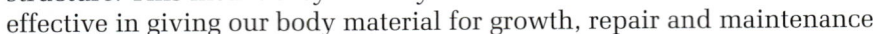

Protein is found in animal products like meat, eggs, cheese, fish and milk. It is also found in **Quorn**. Chemically, these proteins have high **biological value** because of their chemical structure. This means they are very effective in giving our body material for growth, repair and maintenance.

Other foods such as nuts, wheat products and lentils also supply protein. They have lower biological value compared to proteins from animals and Quorn. To improve their biological value these need to be eaten with other proteins.

Protein is a valuable component in manufacturing because of its chemical make up. Proteins, such as egg white, can be whisked so they stretch and trap air. This increases the volume of products like desserts. Proteins also **coagulate** (or set) on heating and hold other ingredients firmly in place in the filling. One example of this would be eggs in quiche filling.

Fats

Fats are divided into yellow fats (butter, margarines and spreads), white fats (such as lard), white vegetable fats and oils. Their chemical make up means that fats are solid at **ambient temperature** and oils are liquid.

Fats combined with proteins are meat fats, milk and dairy fats. Products such as cakes, biscuits, salad dressings and confectionery, for example, chocolate also contain fats.

Chemically, fats supply energy very effectively. More than twice as much energy comes from fat than from the same amount of sugar, starch or protein.

Fat is a very effective food component. Fats give flavour, texture, colour and moistness to many products: for example, crisps, cakes and pastries. Fat also assists in processing as in frying, creaming or shortening.

Sugars and Starches

There are many different types of sugars: white or golden granulated, brown sugars and syrups, fruit sugar (fructose) and glucose. Starches include potatoes, bread, flour, rice and pasta.

Chemically, starches provide energy and other important nutrients, vitamins and minerals. Sugars, however, only provide energy.

Starchy **carbohydrates** are useful food components as they are versatile, process easily and mix with other food groups in lots of tasty combinations such as rice and curry, potato salad, potato on cottage pie. Starches thicken products, usually when heated but if the starch is modified it can thicken cold liquids, too.

Sugary carbohydrates are added to many foods, some savoury, to add sweetness, bulk, extend shelf-life and help texture. Examples include ketchups, cakes and, ice creams.

Written Question

Spend about 10 minutes answering the following question. You will need some paper and something to write with.

This question is about the physical and chemical make up of fats and carbohydrates.

i) Briefly describe a) the different types of fat and b) how fats affect the function of a food product. *(4 marks)*

ii) Name the two groups of carbohydrates and identify the roles they play in food products. *(6 marks)*

Topic 1 Study Guide 3 — Food Materials and Components (1)

Here's what you need to know...

about manipulating food materials and components to create a desired effect.

See *Design & Make It! Food Technology* Revised pages 112–113 (104–105 earlier edition).

KEYWORDS
Do you know what the following terms mean?
- Manipulation
- Stability
- Emulsification
- Nutrition
- Function
- Performance

WWW.
Go to:
www.foodtech.org.uk/fscience/index.html

Manipulating Food Materials and Components

The ingredients of a basic food product can be altered slightly to improve its qualities. For example, it can be given more 'bite': more **mouthfeel**, or texture. It can be made less **bland** by adding different colours or flavours. It can be made stronger, more intensely flavoured, by increasing the amount of a particular ingredient.

Changing Texture, Flavour and Colour

Food products can have their texture changed by *manipulating* their components. For example:
- using crunchy food components such as nuts, grains, large sugar crystals.
- using sticky components such as syrup, jam, or melted chocolate.
- using crisp components such as raw apples, or crushed biscuits.

Food products can also be given dominant flavours or colours by selecting certain components: green peppers, ginger spice, treacle or fresh raspberry juice, for example.

Changing Stability

Food components can be manipulated to help combinations remain *stable*. For example, the egg yolk in mayonnaise keeps the oil mixed into the dressing, when normally it would separate out over time. Keeping oil and water mixed together like this is known as *emulsification*.

Food components can be manipulated to prevent natural change. For example, the citric acid content of lemons can be used to prevent apple, banana and pear slices from going brown in fruit salad.

Changing Nutrition, Function and Performance

Nutritional manipulation means changing the **nutritional value** of a product. It involves adding extra vitamins, as in 'high vitamin C' fruit cordials.

Functional manipulation changes the functions of food components. It involves using **additives** and making process changes such as whipping, as in 'soft scoop' ice cream.

Performance manipulation changes the performance of food components. It involves using additives, for example, to extend the shelf-life of bread.

Written Question

Spend about 9 minutes answering the following question. You will need some paper and something to write with.

A vegetable curry was prepared by a development chef for a 'tasting'. The recipe used has been recorded accurately. After the tasting the responses indicated that the curry was not 'strong' enough, the texture was lacking 'bite' and the colour was too 'bland'.

a) Define the terms bite, bland and strong, as related to the curry. *(3 marks)*
b) Here is a list of ingredients available to the development chef: **i)** chilli powder, **ii)** flaked almonds, **iii)** orange peppers. Select from this list the appropriate ingredients to help improve each of the three qualities lacking in the curry: bite, colour blandness and strength. Explain your choices briefly. *(6 marks)*

17

Topic 1 Study Guide 4   Food Materials and Components (1)

Here's what you need to know...

about ratios and proportions in recipes.

See *Design & Make It! Food Technology* Revised pages 59, 72 (51, 64 earlier edition).

KEYWORDS
Do you know what the following terms mean?
- Ratios
- Proportions
- Basic recipe

What are Ratios and Proportions?

A recipe that included a list of ingredients that just said 'flour, sugar and butter' would not be usable. A recipe needs to include the exact amounts, e.g. 100g of flour, 50g of butter and 25g of sugar. These exact amounts are known as the **quantities**. Quantities clearly show the **proportions** of ingredients that make up a recipe.

The **ratio** of ingredients describes the relationship between the proportions, e.g. 4 parts flour to 2 parts butter to 1 part sugar. This helps make it easier to scale basic recipes up in order to make a larger quantity. Changing the ratio will change the food product being made.

Adapting Basic Recipes

A basic recipe is a reliable, repeatable, small scale working recipe for a product such as a cake, biscuit, sauce or pastry. It is sometimes referred to as a standard recipe. A basic recipe can be **scaled up** for **batch production**.

Pastry ratios
A **basic recipe** for shortcrust pastry shows that the main ingredients are plain white flour and fat, such as hard margarine. However much is made, the fat amount is 50% of the flour weight, a ratio of 1 to 2. If the ratio of fat to flour was increased the product would become what is known as flaky or puff pastry.

Cake ratios
In cake making, the method of production often depends on the proportion of fat used. If the ratio is equal parts fat to sugar to flour the method is 'all in one' or 'creaming'. A lower ratio of fat would probably use a 'rubbing in' method.

Sauce ratios
Sauces use **thickeners** such as cornflour or wheat flour. If the proportions of flour to the amount of liquid are increased the sauce becomes thicker when hot and sets very solid when cold. Sauces can be pouring thickness, coating thickness or binding thickness.

Written Question

Spend about 6 minutes answering the following question. You will need some paper and something to write with.

A manufacturer requires a white roux sauce to pour on to a vegetable.

a) Copy out and complete the recipe details for the food technologists to try in the test kitchen.
   500ml milk
   25g.......... and 25g..........   *(2 marks)*

b) Explain why it would be a good basic recipe.   *(4 marks)*

Topic 1 Study Guide 5 — Food Materials and Components (1)

Here's what you need to know...

about the use of alternative ingredients in food products.

See *Design & Make It! Food Technology* Revised pages 80–82.

KEYWORDS

Do you know what the following terms mean?
- Alternative ingredients
- Quorn
- Soya TVP
- Meat analogues

WWW.
Go to:
www.quorn.com/uk/index.htm
www.tivall.co.uk

Alternative Ingredients

Alternative ingredients are food materials and components that can be used to replace existing materials and components. This can reduce costs and/or make the product suitable for different diets. For example, **Quorn**™ and **soya TVP** (textured vegetable protein) are alternative protein foods. They are known as **meat analogues** – vegetable products that resemble meat.

Flavouring components and ingredients often need to be added to Quorn and soya.

Quorn

Quorn is the result of **new product development (NPD)**. It is made from **mycoprotein**, which is a kind of fungus, like mushroom. It contains protein, can be processed as mince, fillets or chunks and has a similar taste and texture to meat products – without containing any meat. This makes it suitable for vegetarian diets. It is a healthy product due to the fact that it is low in fat and contains some **dietary fibre**, unlike meat. Food technologists have already developed a range of ready meals based on Quorn.

Soya

Soya is also used to create meat analogues. Soya beans can be processed to create flour, milk and TVP (textured vegetable protein) chunks. TVP can resemble minced beef, chicken chunks, burgers and sausages for vegetarian food products. It can also be used with real meat to extend the meaty part of a product. TVP can be dried and then be **rehydrated** easily. One-pot snacks are a popular food product based on TVP that are enjoyed by meat eaters and vegetarians alike.

Soya beans are very versitile. For example, they can be used to make dairy-free chocolate desserts that can be eaten by people who are allergic to dairy products.

500g pork sausages
300g onions
500ml rich dark gravy
800g cooked mashed potatoes

Written Question

Spend about 10 minutes answering the following question. You will need some paper and something to write with.

The recipe opposite is used by a manufacturer for a sausage and mash ready meal for kids.

i) Which two meat analogues could be used to replace the pork sausages? *(4 marks)*

ii) Explain two differences these changes could make to the nutritional profile of this product. *(2 marks)*

iii) Suggest and describe one way the manufacturer could compensate for the fact that the meat analogue lacked flavour. *(4 marks)*

Topic 2 Study Guide 1 — Food Materials and Components (2)

Working Characteristics

The **working characteristic** of a food material or component usually means the way it handles or 'functions' during preparation and cooking.

Cooking is the addition of heat, controlled by time and temperature. Cooking can cause working characteristics to change dramatically. Working characteristics can also change when heat is removed in cooling, chilling and freezing *(see Section 2 of this Topic)*.

Here's what you need to know...

about the addition of heat during preparation of food products.

See *Design & Make It! Food Technology* Revised pages 92–93, 96, 111 (84–85, 88, 103 earlier edition).

KEYWORDS
Do you know what the following terms mean?
- Working characteristics
- Coagulation
- Gelatinisation
- Caramelisation

WWW.
Go to:
www.foodtech.org.uk/processing/index.html

Melting, softening, shrinking and solidifying

- Some food components melt when they are heated (e.g. cheese, butter, chocolate) and set when they cool again.
- Some food materials become tender and softer on cooking (e.g. potatoes, pasta and rice).
- Some products shrink when they are heated (such as fish, red meats and chicken).
- Some protein food components become solid or rigid when cooked (eggs and wheat flour protein (**gluten**), for example). This is known as **coagulation**.

Thickening, colouring, and caramelising

- Some starch components expand and thicken liquids when heated. This is known as **gelatinisation**. Examples are cornflour and wheat flour in sauce-making.
- Some products change colour due to heat (e.g. when toasting bread and baking cakes).
- Sugars **caramelise** when heated to give the golden colour and sweetness of many baked products.

Combining, preserving and extending shelf-life

- Some mixture combinations produce short, crumbly crisp textures when heated (e.g. the flour and fat mixture in pastry).
- Some mixtures of food components combine to give light open textures when heated (for example, creamed margarine and sugar in cakes, or whisked eggs and sugar in swiss roll).
- Some food components **preserve** other products when heated (sugar in jam, for example).
- Some components extend **shelf-life** when heated – such as fat and sugar cooked together in cakes and biscuits.

Written Question

Spend about 8 minutes answering the following question. You will need some paper and something to write with.

The ways different foods behave when cooked are varied and complex.

If rice, sugar, milk and butter were to be used together in a food product, explain what you would expect their function to be as they cooked.

To answer, complete the following sentences.

i)   I think the rice would…   *(2 marks)*
ii) I think the sugar would…   *(2 marks)*
iii) I think the milk would…   *(2 marks)*
iv) I think the butter would…   *(2 marks)*

Topic 2 Study Guide 2 — Food Materials and Components (2)

Here's what you need to know...

about the removal of heat during preparation of food products.

See *Design & Make It! Food Technology* Revised pages 68–70 (60, 62 earlier edition).

KEYWORDS
Do you know what the following terms mean?
- Cooling
- Chilling
- Cook-chill
- Freezing

WWW.
Go to:
www.foodtech.org.uk/processing/index.html

This section is about what happens to the **working characteristics** of food materials when heat is removed. (Section 1 of this Topic looks at what happens when heat is applied.)

What is Removal of Heat?
Removal of heat from food materials and components is known as **cooling**, **chilling** or **freezing**. It can be a process carried out after cooking.

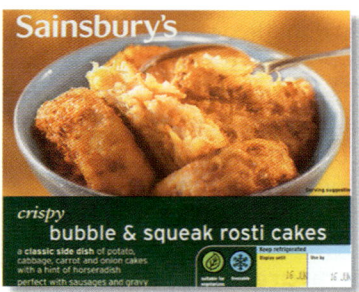

Cooling
Cooling is a process required after cooking and before wrapping. Food products are cooled as rapidly as possible. Cooling takes products from oven temperature down to **5–8°C**.

Chilling
Chilling is the rapid removal of heat to a temperature in the range of **1–4°C**. This:
- extends the keeping qualities of many foods.
- reduces the activity of **microbes**.
- makes some food components harder or firmer, for example, cheese, fats.

Rapid chilling of cooked foods and then storage at **1–2°C** is known as **cook-chill**. Cook-chill is a widely used method. It allows fresh products with a variety of food components to be stored just above freezing for up to four days.

Freezing
Freezing is the removal of heat to temperatures well below freezing point (0°C).
The usual temperature range for freezing is **–18°C to –29°C**. Removal of heat to this degree:
- causes most food components to freeze solid and keep for many months.
- does not destroy **nutrients** – they remain unchanged until thawed.

When things freeze, water in the cells expands and may burst the cell walls, changing structure and texture. Rapid freezing causes less damage to cells than gradual freezing.

Written Question

Spend about 10 minutes answering the following question. You will need some paper and something to write with.

Compare the reasons a food manufacturer might consider for using chilling or cook-chilling rather than freezing for processing some food products. Make particular reference to the needs of the consumer. *(10 marks)*

Topic 2 Study Guide 3 — Food Materials and Components (2)

Here's what you need to know...

about controlling the temperature of food products during processing and storage.

See *Design & Make It! Food Technology* Revised page 98 (90 earlier edition).

KEYWORDS
Do you know what the following terms mean?
- Temperature control
- Control testing
- Food probes
- Shelf temperature
- Ambient temperature

Controlling the Temperature

It is necessary to **control the temperature** of food products **precisely** during processing and storage prior to production, in transport, in shops and when the consumer stores the food in cupboards, fridges and freezers. This is essential to ensure products are **consistent** and **safe** for the consumer to eat.

Control testing

If temperatures are not correct during food processing, there are usually **systems** to alert people, such as alarm bells or flashing lights. Freezer storerooms are an example, where an alarm may sound if the temperature becomes too warm. The system of checking and monitoring temperatures in food production and storage is known as **control testing**.

Controlling high temperatures

High temperature processing (between 100°C and 121°C) such as canning is likely to soften products and alter the flavour (according to the juice used in the can). Careful temperature control is needed to ensure that the colour of the product remains fairly stable and the reduction in **nutritional value** and loss of **water-soluble vitamins** are kept to a minimum.

Controlling low temperatures

Freezing food uses very low temperatures (i.e. between −20°C and −30°C). This severe cold can alter the texture of the food. Reasonably juicy products such as tomatoes, soft fruits and vegetables need to be frozen quickly. Accurate control of rapid freezing is needed to ensure the water in the product forms only tiny crystals that do not damage the cell walls. Slower freezing rates allow larger crystals to grow, which can burst the cell walls.

Food materials and components containing lots of water such as salad leaves cannot be frozen successfully. Dry products such as cakes and breads freeze perfectly. Freezing does not affect the **nutritional value** of foods to any great extent.

Taking the temperature

Food probes are used to record the temperatures food reach during cooking, processing and during storage. Some food probes are hand-held devices, others are built into machines. A hand-held food probe is inserted into the food or between food packs to get an accurate temperature.

Shelf temperatures are the temperature of open storage shelves, and will vary according to the season between about 18°C and 22°C. **Ambient temperature** is air temperature, usually around 20°C indoors. Shelf and indoor ambient temperatures in the food industry are measured and controlled by **thermostats** that trigger heating and cooling systems to keep temperatures in the correct range.

Written Question

Spend about 11 minutes answering the following question. You will need some paper and something to write with.

a) State what would happen if control tests were not carried out during processing or storage of food products. *(3 marks)*

b) When discussing the preservation of food products a food technologist states:

'Canning food products means that the contents undergo very high temperature so some changes are to be expected.'

Say if each of the following changes would be expected as a result of canning, and why, or why not.
i) a change in price.
ii) a change in nutrients.
iii) a change in texture.
iv) a change in name. *(8 marks)*

Topic 2 Study Guide 4 — Food Materials and Components (2)

Here's what you need to know...

about the effects of acids, alkalis and micro-organisms.

See *Design & Make It! Food Technology* Revised pages 94–95, 96–97 (86–87, 88–89 earlier edition).

KEYWORDS
Do you know what the following terms mean?
- Acids
- Alkalis
- Micro-organisms

WWW.
Go to:
www.foodtech.org.uk/fscience/index.html

The Effects of Acids, Alkalis and Micro-organisms

As well as temperature, many other factors affect food production. These include *acids*, *alkalis* and *micro-organisms*. These can change the texture, finish, appearance and storage requirements of a product. These features are often what provide the distinctive features of the **product profile**.

Acids

Acids are products with a low **pH** of between **1 and 7**. They can help create the right conditions for the prevention of **enzymic browning**. For example, citric acid in the form of lemon juice is used in the preparation of apples in fruit salads. This prevents the surface of the apple slices browning and so improves the appearance of the fruit in the salad.

Tartaric acids are used as **raising agents** in baking powder. Scones and biscuits owe their open texture to the use of acid raising agents.

Acids can achieve a desired special texture. The marshmallow texture of pavlova meringue is achieved by adding vinegar (acetic acid) while preparing the meringue.

Acids are very frequently used for achieving a desirable 'tangy' acidic or sharp flavour to stimulate the digestive juices when dining, such as in dressings for salads, lemon flavoured desserts, raspberry topping. Regulating the acidity is vital in many products from chewy sweets to jams and fizzy drinks.

Alkalis

The crackled appearance on biscuits, such as ginger nuts, is due to the addition of a small amount of the alkali sodium bicarbonate to the recipe. It acts as a raising agent in some products such as cakes and gingerbread. Alkalis can taste soapy so they are used with care.

Micro-organisms

Micro-organisms are yeasts, moulds and bacteria. They are used to create colour, flavour and texture in foods.

- Yeasts help ferment products, act as raising agents and produce alcohol.
- Moulds give flavour to cheeses such as blue cheese.
- Bacteria creates creamy yoghurts.

Written Question

Spend about 4 minutes answering the following question. You will need some paper and something to write with.

A salad dressing is made from the following ingredients:
- Sunflower oil
- Sea salt
- Water
- Black pepper
- Pinch of sugar

The mixture is prepared by shaking vigorously.

Sensory analysis gives the following results:

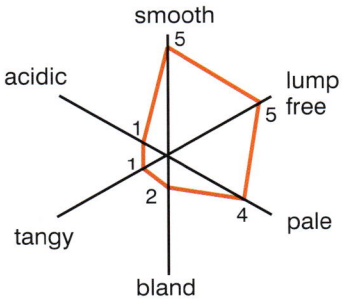

This shows that the dressing is not very tangy, and not at all acidic.

Suggest a range of ingredients that could be used to create a more acidic and tangy flavour. *(4 marks)*

Topic 2 Study Guide 5 — Food Materials and Components (2)

Here's what you need to know...

about the use of 'smart' materials in food production.

See *Design & Make It! Food Technology* Revised pages 9, 93 (85 earlier edition).

KEYWORDS

Do you know what the following terms mean?
- Smart foods
- Modified starches
- Fat replacers
- Sweeteners
- Functional foods
- Encapsulation
- Bulk sweeteners

WWW.
Go to:
www.olean.com
www.nutrition.org.uk

What are 'Smart' Food Materials'?

Smart materials are designed to behave in a different way from natural food ingredients and components. Their properties and characteristics have been deliberately changed in some way. The main types of smart ingredients are:

- Modified starches
- Fat replacers
- Sweeteners
- Functional ingredients
- Encapsulated ingredients

Modified starches

Over time the **consistency** and quality of a food product that has been made using starch as an ingredient can start to deteriorate. Modified starches are used to provide consistent results matched to the particular requirements of the product, e.g. when a product needs an extended shelf-life. Starch can be modified by physical means (e.g. heating), or the use of chemicals (e.g. **oxidisation**).

Modified starches are often found in salad dressings, instant desserts, fruit pie fillings, 'pot' snacks and cook-chill meals.

Fat replacers

Smart materials can be developed to **perform** instead of another ingredient. There is a lot of scientific research into fat replacers – materials that will perform just like fat but not contain any calories. 'Olestra' is an American fat replacer that is not absorbed by the body and has no calories. It is not yet available in the UK. These products could help reduce the number of people who are obese, as long as any side effects are not judged to be harmful.

Sweeteners

Saccharin is an example of an artificial sweetener. As it is many times sweeter than sugar it need only be used in tiny amounts. It is therefore widely used in diet drinks. Sorbitol is a **bulk sweetener** used in sugar-free sweets.

Functional ingredients

Functional ingredients are those that add extra health-giving properties to a product. Two common products are spreads that lower **cholesterol**, and pre- and pro-biotic milk drinks and yoghurts that improve **microbial balance** and help maintain a healthy digestive system.

Many food products contain added **nutrients**. This is usually to replace those lost in processing, but they are sometimes added to products that would not normally have those particular nutrients, such as calcium in orange juice.

Encapsulated ingredients

When an ingredient is encapsulated it is coated in a shell that prevents it from **interacting** with other ingredients or the surrounding atmosphere. At the appropriate moment the ingredient is released by compression, dissolving, breaking or melting. Encapsulation can be used to:

- enhance flavour, colour and nutritional content.
- help produce **consistent** products.
- aid **preservation**.

Jelly beans are a good example of the use of encapsulated flavours that are released when the product is bitten. Encapsulated vitamins can be added to sports drinks and snack bars.

Written Question

Spend about 10 minutes answering the following question. You will need some paper and something to write with.

Food technologists and scientists can now use smart materials in response to a need. They know that some smart materials make things possible which were not previously possible.

Explain if, and how, it is now possible to create the following products.

i) A product that will thicken cold milk so that thick milk shakes can be made at home.
(5 marks)

ii) An almost fat free cake which looks delicious and is not fattening. *(5 marks)*

Topic 3 Study Guide 1 — Industrial Food Product Design (1)

Here's what you need to know...

about investigating products and their specific target groups.

See *Design & Make It! Food Technology* Revised pages 78, 116–117, 140, 146–147 (70, 108–109, 132, 138–139 earlier edition).

KEYWORDS

Do you know what the following terms mean?
- Market research
- Target group
- Consumer
- Lifestyle

WWW.
Go to:
www.j-sainsbury.co.uk/
education/tasteofsuccess/
secondary.htm

Meeting the Customer's Needs

Manufacturers spend a great deal of time and money on **market research** and the analysis of:
- changing needs, preferences and eating patterns of **target groups**.
- how well existing food products meet the **consumer**'s needs.

Consumers can be grouped according to their likely needs, income and lifestyle. Typical target groups are:

Families
Families eat together less frequently now and eat out of the home on a more regular basis. Less time is available for preparing meals. Families may be willing to pay more for food products that save them time, especially if both parents are working. **Working parents** will have more money, but less time. The increase in demand for ready meals, part-prepared food, cook-chill and frozen foods is seen in all major supermarkets.

Healthy eaters
Consumers interested in **healthy eating** want less fat, sugar and salt in their diets. Product ranges such as 'Eat Smart', and 'Perfectly Balanced', have been developed for the 'healthy eating' market.

Slimmers
Slimmers increasingly look for calorie counted and **reduced calorie** products from ranges such as the 'Go Ahead', 'Lean Cuisine' or 'Count On Us' products.

Children
Children are a **target group**. They are attracted to food products with brightly coloured packaging, fun shaped food or products relating to current films or TV programmes. Concern about establishing healthy eating patterns for children has brought about efforts to make these products using less salt, lower fat, little added sugar and no additives.

Vegetarians
There are many more **vegetarians** in the UK than there were 20 years ago. To meet their needs product ranges based on vegetables, pulses and meat substitutes have been developed.

Other cultures
The wider **cultural mix** of UK citizens and consumers who now travel more, or have strong family links with other cultures, are the newest target group. They want authentic dishes and ingredients from around the world. Foods using herbs, spices, ingredients and processes from India, Thailand, China and Mexico and all parts of the world are now styled and successfully marketed.

Written Question

Spend about 10 minutes answering the following question.
You will need some paper and something to write with

Existing food products are designed for specific target consumer groups. Identify two typical target consumer groups. For each group, give three reasons why they have different needs to the other. Give examples of food products manufactured especially for each group. *(10 marks)*

Topic 3 Study Guide 2 — Industrial Food Product Design (1)

Here's what you need to know...

about investigating customer views.

See *Design & Make It! Food Technology* Revised pages 116-117, 125, 138–139 (108–109, 117, 130–131, earlier edition).

KEYWORDS

Do you know what the following terms mean?
- Sensory characteristics
- Nutritional information

WWW.
Go to:
www.j-sainsbury.co.uk/
education/tasteofsuccess/
secondary.htm

What the Food Technologist Thinks

Manufacturers gain a lot of information from studying food products that already exist. They **analyse** their physical and nutritional **characteristics** and use this to develop new recipes suited to specific **target groups**. For example, a team of food technologists might consider:

- Price range – is it aimed at the economy, mid-range or luxury/gourmet markets?
- Portion size – how many individuals will the product serve?
- Ingredients – what is it made from, and in what proportions?
- Appearance/presentation – the food product's shape, colour and finish.
- Cooking instructions – different tools and appliances required, how long and at what temperature?
- Serving suggestions – what other food products can it be served with to make a meal?
- Storage conditions – where the product should be kept – in a cupboard, a refrigerator or a freezer?
- **Shelf-life** – how long can it be kept in a cupboard, fridge or freezer?
- Packaging – is it informative, attractive, stimulating, **environmentally friendly**, etc?

What the Consumer Says

After describing an existing product in this way, the next step is to consider how successful it is. To do this, food technologists need to keep up to date with what consumers think of the products they are studying. They need to find out the preferences of different target groups in terms of a product's:

- **sensory characteristics** – if they like its appearance, smell, taste and texture.
- **nutritional information** – how well does it meet their needs for healthy, vegetarian or other special dietary requirements?
- cost – is the price right? Would they buy the product more often if it was cheaper, or spend more on a luxury version?
- portion size – is there too much or too little in the package?
- availability – is the product sold in the right locations – where consumers want and expect to find it?

Food Product Development

After carefully considering all the available information, the food technologists can then start to explore how a product might be improved, or changed in some way, to make it more appealing to a wider or different **consumer group**.

Written Question

Spend about 6 minutes answering the following question. You will need some paper and something to write with.

A team of food technologists are studying a range of existing cook-chill products to identify possible ways in which they could be developed to make them more appealing to elderly people. Name three features of the products they might study in detail. Explain why and how they could be developed to appeal to the elderly.

(6 marks)

Topic 3 Study Guide 3 — Industrial Food Product Design (1)

Tell Us About Yourself

What do people want? When and where do they buy? What would they like? Finding out the views and preferences of potential customers is a very important part of any food business. This is known as **market research**.

The main methods used in market research are **questionnaires**, **interviews** and **statistical data**. Gathering information from a wide range of sources gives a fuller picture than information from a single source. **ICT** (Information and Communication Technology) has greatly enhanced the way in which this can be done.

Surveys

Questionnaires are used to gather factual information about sample groups of people, such as age, income, shops they visit, what they buy, etc. To learn more about people's opinions, personal interviews are conducted.

Sometimes a market research team will design and undertake their own specific **survey**. On other occasions they may be able to use more general information collected by national research agencies, such as **MORI** (which stands for Market & Opinion Research International) who provide information about the **trends** in the food business.

A Rewarding Experience

Information about **buying patterns** can also be obtained from analysing sales data. Customer loyalty and reward cards are a way of collecting data about what people buy, how much they buy, what they buy with it and when they buy it. **Barcoding** is another way of obtaining this information.

Are You Being Watched?

Internet shopping provides extensive data on users' interests and buying patterns. As part of the process of buying something, 'online' customers are often asked for information about themselves. **E-mails** can be sent inviting users to complete **electronic questionnaires**, significantly cutting the costs of printing and postage. Records can also be kept showing which web pages have been viewed and re-visited the most.

Electronic Storage

When all this information has been gathered it is stored electronically in a computer **database** or **spreadsheet**. These enable complex analysis and cross-referencing to be undertaken quickly and easily. It also means that the data can automatically be presented as graphs and charts, and is therefore easier to understand.

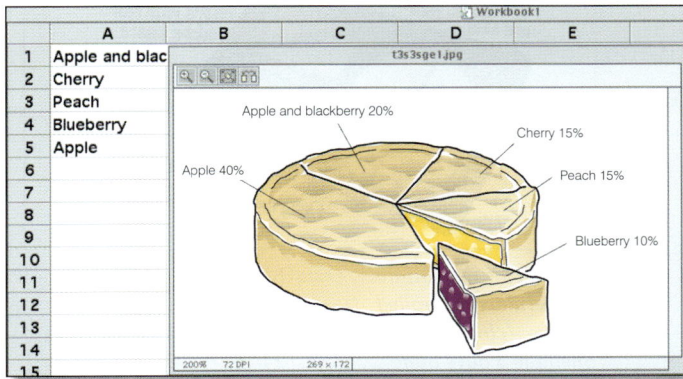

Here's what you need to know...

about gathering information from a range of different sources.

See *Design & Make It! Food Technology* Revised pages 16–17 (8–9 earlier edition).

KEYWORDS

Do you know what the following terms mean?
- Market research
- MORI (Market & Opinion Research International)

WWW.
Go to:
www.mori.com
www.bmesonline.org.uk

Written Question

Spend about 6 minutes answering the following question. You will need some paper and something to write with.

A food technologist creating a new product needs to find out more about the target group's views, preferences and shopping and eating habits. Choose a target group and explain three methods that could be used to gather appropriate information for the food technologist. *(6 marks)*

Topic 3 Study Guide 4 — Industrial Food Product Design (1)

Here's what you need to know...

about design criteria and product formulation.

See *Design & Make It! Food Technology* Revised pages 68–69, 105–106 (60–61, 98–99 earlier edition).

KEYWORDS
Do you know what the following terms mean?
- Design criteria
- Design specification
- Product formulation
- Prototype
- Product specification

www.
Go to:
www.j-sainsbury.co.uk/education/tasteofsuccess/secondary.htm

Design Criteria

After a team of food technologists and market researchers have studied a range of existing products and identified consumers' views, preferences and habits, a clear statement of the **target group** and the type of product required is given, e.g. 'There is a need for a new gluten-free chocolate biscuit product aimed at people who have an allergy to wheat.'

A list of **design criteria** can then be considered. These criteria help guide the **development process** and ensure that a new product will successfully appeal to a particular **target group**. For example:
- price range – is the new product aimed at the economy, mid-range or luxury/gourmet markets?
- portion size – how many individual people will the new product serve?
- ingredients – are there any special dietary or cultural requirements?
- appearance/presentation – what sort of preferences for shape, colour and finish does the target market have?
- cooking (reheating) instructions – any limitations on the different tools and appliances that need to be used?

Design Specification

The **design specification** follows on from the design criteria that have been considered. For example:
- price-range – the product must come into the mid-range market.
- portion size – the product must serve four people.
- ingredients – the product must have a pastry case.
- cooking instructions – the product must not take longer than 30 minutes to prepare in the home.

Food Product Formulation

The food technologists can then begin the process of new **product formulation**. They will use **annotated sketches**, experiment with different ingredients and flavours and use computers to establish the basis of a possible product. Ideas are regularly discussed, evaluated and reviewed.

At the end of this stage of the process the new product development team will identify and list the detailed requirements for making the final product **prototype**. This list of detailed requirements is called the **product specification**. For example: the pastry must be a round, golden brown, short-crust pastry case with a fluted edge.

From the product specification it should be possible for someone else to make the product prototype **exactly** as described.

Written Question

Spend about 8 minutes answering the following question.
You will need some paper and something to write with.

i) On the right is a sketch for a new food product, based on a design specification. Study the sketch and suggest four statements that might have appeared in the specification. *(4 marks)*

ii) Suggest two changes that could be made to the design specification that would make the food product more suitable for children aged 4–7 years. *(4 marks)*

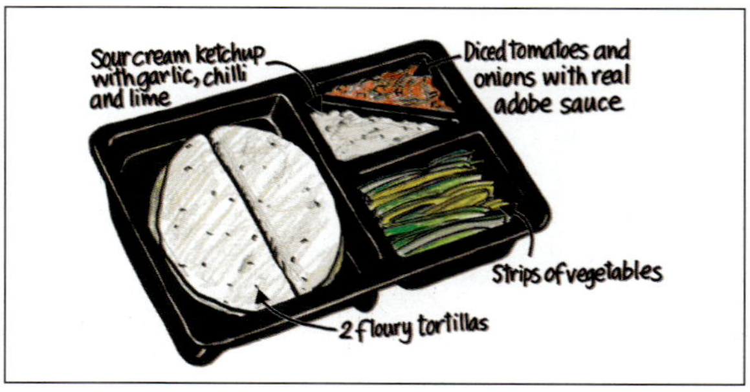

Suitable for vegetarians. Temperature controlled storage – chiller cabinet 2°C. Shelf life 5 days from production.

Black rigid, pre-formed, plastic tray. Overall dimensions 18cm x 24cm. Heat sealed film covering.

Topic 3 Study Guide 5 | Industrial Food Product Design (1)

Here's what you need to know...

about developing and testing food product prototypes.

See *Design & Make It! Food Technology* Revised page 119 (111 earlier edition).

KEYWORDS
Do you know what the following terms mean?
- Prototype
- Product development
- Manufacturing specification

www.
Go to:
www.nutrition.org.uk

Testing and Improving the Prototype

After a new food product has been **formulated**, **prototype** products need to be made. These can then be tested, evaluated and modified by the food technologists, manufacturer, retailer and **consumer panel**. This section is about the aspects of the product that are tested at this stage. The methods used to conduct the tests are covered in Topic 4, Section 1.

What Needs to be Tested

Many changes can take place during this stage of further **product development**. **Modifications** and **reformulation** are likely to involve the following aspects:

- **sensory characteristics** – may need to be improved or changed depending on the views of experts.
- **ingredients** – may need to be altered if problems are likely to occur in obtaining sufficient quantities of particular ingredients.
- **processing systems** – to speed up the production line or permit greater output. They may be changed to create a special effect such as increased volume by 'whipping' instead of stirring.
- **health and safety** concerns – may mean a risk or hazard is indicated and therefore changes will be needed to control times, temperatures or other factors.
- **nutritional information** – may need to be adjusted to satisfy the needs of a particular target market.
- use of **additives** – may need to be reduced to create a more easily processed product, or make a more acceptable ingredients listing.
- **shelf-life**, packaging, reheating or cooking instructions – these all require considerable testing to ensure that they are accurate for the product and acceptable to the consumer.
- **costing** factors – these are vital to the success of a food product and need to be carefully considered when presenting a food product to the retail sector. Changes to the product can affect the **commercial viability** of a product.
- **design** issues (e.g. environmental and social factors) – need to be taken into consideration, and the product modified as appropriate.

Manufacturing Specification

When the product prototype has been finalised the **manufacturing specification** can be prepared. This gives exact details of the ingredients and processes needed for the manufacturer to make exact replicas of the final prototype in large quantities. This is described in more detail in Section 2 of Topic 4.

Written Question

Spend about 6 minutes answering the following question. You will need some paper and something to write with

A group of food technologists are developing a new food product based on a three-sectioned ready made product consisting of sliced meat with sauce, potatoes and mixed vegetables. It is aimed at older people who prefer traditional food.

Identify three aspects that might be modified if a prototype version of this product was being tested. *(6 marks)*

29

Topic 4 Study Guide 1 — Industrial Food Product Design (2)

Here's what you need to know...

about testing food product prototypes.

See *Design & Make It! Food Technology* Revised pages 68–69, 112–113, 114–115 (60–61, 104–105, 106–107 earlier edition).

KEYWORDS
Do you know what the following terms mean?
- Prototype
- Quantitative tests
- Qualitative tests
- Sensory analysis
- Product profile
- Comparison tests
- Laboratory tests
- Nutritional tests
- Production tests
- Key characteristics

WWW.
Go to:
www.nutrition.org.uk

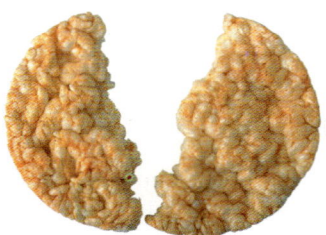

Testing Prototypes

Before any food product is put into final production, **prototypes** are developed through **testing**. The results of the testing provide information on which to base decisions and changes. Testing prototypes is essential if products are to be **safe**, **conform to specification** and maintain their **quality**.

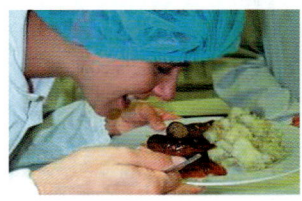

Testing Methods

The testing can be carried out by **quantitative measurements** such as sizes of depth, width, volume, weight, cost or **nutritional data**.

Other testing may be **hedonic testing** – people's general likes and dislikes, or **qualitative tests** such as **sensory analysis** that examine specific qualities. Sensory analysis is undertaken using tasters who may record scores for sensory **criteria** such as crispness, sweetness on to a **product profile** web chart.

Comparison tests by pairs testing, ranking and rating, or triangle tests may also be carried out. Comparison tests are also known as Difference tests. Such tests are always carried out in carefully controlled environments and the data collected accurately in order to provide sound evidence of **fair testing**.

Laboratory Tests

Laboratories carry out **microbial tests** on prototype food products to find out the numbers and types of bacteria, yeasts and moulds present. **Humidity tests** are done to determine the amount of water in a product, or indeed the dryness of a product, to help forecast the **shelf-life**.

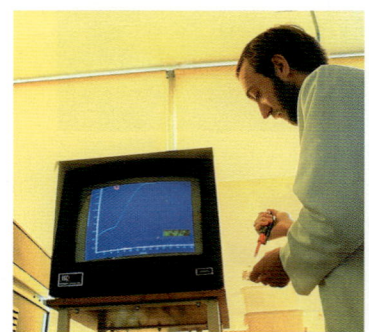

Testing for shelf-life is carried out by observation and not by sampling the product by mouth at all. Other experiments can find out the exact **mould free shelf-life (MFSL)** of a product and thus the 'best before' or 'use-by' date can be specified.

Nutritional testing, using computer nutritional database analysis, could work out all the various nutrients in a **scaled up** recipe for production. Weights are measured and stored ready for printing on packaging so that information for the consumer is accurate.

The **key characteristics** of products may be exactly measured. For example, the stickiness of a malt loaf, the snap point of a biscuit or the amount of vitamin in a breakfast cereal so that specifications about a product are exact and **repeatable**.

Production Testing

Production testing is carried out to discover any problems in making the product in quantity. For example, in maintaining temperature control over a range of processes and movement down the production line.

The sweetness and flavour of a product would be tested to check the exact level of sweetness and the quality of the flavour when made in large amounts.

Test data concerning re-heating times, freezing times and storage temperature are also vital in taking the prototype forward to becoming an actual product.

Written Question

Spend about 9 minutes answering the following question. You will need some paper and something to write with.

A manufacturer of flavoured, sweetened yoghurt has developed an exciting food product prototype.

i) Name and briefly describe a test that might be undertaken to evaluate the flavour of the new product. *(3 marks)*

ii) Name and briefly describe a test that might be undertaken in a laboratory. *(3 marks)*

iii) Name and briefly describe a test that might be undertaken using a computer. *(3 marks)*

| Topic 4 Study Guide 2 | Industrial Food Product Design (2) |

Here's what you need to know...

about preparing a manufacturing specification for a new food product.

See *Design & Make It! Food Technology* Revised pages 18, 34, 46, 118 (11, 26, 38, 110 earlier edition).

KEYWORDS
Do you know what the following term means?
- Manufacturing specification

Manufacturing Specification

The **manufacturing specification** identifies every detail of the making or manufacturing of a food product. It fixes every detail about the product by **documenting** it on paper very clearly. As a result the product can be manufactured by any company, or in any factory, and it would be the same.

Writing the manufacturing specification is the last step in the whole process of **product development**. Before this can be done the food technologists need to consider the processes involved in making **batches** of the products. Exact **repeatability** is an important factor about a food product.

Specifying Processes

The manufacturing specification will need to outline the exact processing methods to be used during manufacture – inspection, washing, sorting, heat treatments such as boiling, simmering, baking, and cooling.

Specifying Ingredients

The manufacturing specification must include full details of the ingredients to be used, the appearance, shape, size and weight, and the processing methods to be used to make the product. Details of any **standard components** will need to be specified as part of the production process. Full information about the packaging design must also be provided.

HACCP

An essential part of any manufacturing specification is a **HACCP** (Hazard Analysis and Critical Control Points) safety specification. Procedures for **quality control** are also included. (These are all covered in more detail in Sections 3, 4 and 5 of this topic).

MANUFACTURING SPECIFICATION
Cauliflower in cheese and ham sauce

Product description:
Florets of cauliflower in a rich and creamy cheese and ham sauce with crunchy topping

Ingredients:
Cauliflower, Boiled ham, Sauce, Topping.

Preparation:
- Clean and trim cauliflower – blanch in boiling water for 7 mins and drain
- Dice boiled ham – strips not more than 1.5 cm by 1 cm

Standard components:
Cheese sauce mix – make up with whole milk
Topping mix - seasoning, white breadcrumbs and cheddar cheese

Process:
- Portion out cauliflower pieces 300–310g into deep rigid foil container (8x15 cm)
- Coat with 500g sauce mix made up to 'pouring' thickness, combined with 80g strips ham
- Layer with 150g topping mix
- Cover with foiled paperboard lid and add pre-printed card sleeve
- Scan data: production line, use by date, product code, factory

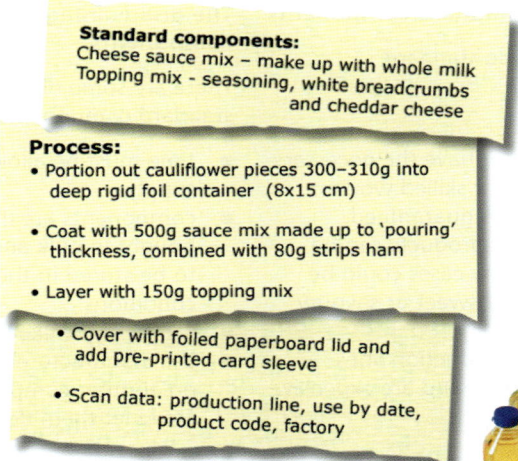

Written Question

Spend about 8 minutes answering the following question. You will need some paper and something to write with.

A manufacturing specification includes precise information about ingredients, quantities, production processes and safety procedures. Explain why a manufacturing specification is required for a food product.

(8 marks)

Topic 4 Study Guide 3 — Industrial Food Product Design (2)

Here's what you need to know...

about the use of standard components in food product manufacture.

See *Design & Make It! Food Technology* Revised page 144 (136 earlier edition).

KEYWORDS

Do you know what the following term means?
- Standard components

Standard Components

Standard components are **pre-prepared** items used in food production. They are made at a different time, and often at a different place by another company. Common examples are:

- fruit fillings for pies
- sauces
- stuffings
- pizza bases
- spice mixtures
- pre-shaped pastry
- coatings
- ready mixes of ingredients
- toppings
- pre-prepared vegetables

Ensuring the Standard

Using standard components helps ensure a **consistent** final product because they are of a standard quality, i.e. standard weight, size, shape, intensity of flavour, and accurate in **ratio** of ingredients.

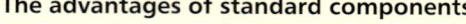

As well as saving time and money, standard components also help **quality control** by guaranteeing a consistent and reliable quality. They can often be made cheaply by a specialist supplier because they can be manufactured in very large numbers on a dedicated **production line**.

Decisions about the suitable use of standard components need to be made at the food product **prototype** stage. Precise and accurate **manufacturing specifications** are absolutely essential.

The advantages of standard components

Manufacturers may use standard components:

- to save time.
- because they do not have the necessary specific machinery or skilled workers.
- so that the quality is guaranteed.
- so a wider range of products can be produced, e.g. pastry cases could be used for a variety of sweet or savoury fillings.
- because complex production lines take up a lot of space and are expensive to set up.

The disadvantages of standard components

There are some disadvantages to using standard components:

- time must be allowed for ordering and supply.
- components are usually bought in bulk and have to be stored in the right conditions.
- can be more expensive.
- the manufacturer is relying on another company that could let them down.

Written Question

Answer the following question on lined paper. Do not spend more than about 8 minutes writing your answer.

Pre-manufactured standard components are sometimes used when decorating large-scale celebration cakes. Give three examples of standard components that could be used in decorating these cakes and explain why they would be used. *(8 marks)*

32

Topic 4 Study Guide 4 — Industrial Food Product Design (2)

Here's what you need to know...

about how quality control procedures are identified and applied in the food manufacturing process.

See *Design & Make It! Food Technology* Revised pages 54, 120 (46, 112 earlier edition).

KEYWORDS
Do you know what the following terms mean?
- Quality control
- Quality assurance

Quality Counts

The need for **consistent** quality is very important in the food manufacturing process, from the ingredients to the final packaging. Regular checks on quality are needed to ensure that each product in a batch looks and tastes the same, and is safe to eat. **Legal requirements** now make it essential for producers to have evidence of their quality systems.

Quality covers many aspects of production, and includes things such as:

- freedom from **contamination**
- maintenance of **mould free shelf-life**
- protection by packaging and an assumption that food products are **safe**.

What is a Quality Control System?

Quality control involves a series of methods used to check products as they are made. In most cases it would take too long to inspect *every* item on a **production line**. For this reason a **sample** is examined – one in every hundred, or thousand perhaps, or once a minute, or maybe half-hour, depending on the product. The results of the test are recorded and compared. If they become regularly unsatisfactory then the production process is stopped. The problem needs to be sorted out before too many **sub-standard** products are produced.

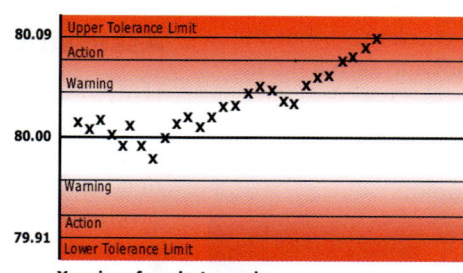

X = size of product sample

Using ICT

Some quality control checks will be undertaken and recorded by production line workers – checks on protective clothing for example. **Computer-controlled** systems are frequently used for machine processes. Computers can supply **feedback** quickly, they can process large amounts of information at high speed and keep logs of data over long periods of time which can be easily accessed and analysed.

Planning for Quality

The various quality control checklists that are needed are identified and planned during the development of the food product **prototype**. They are then written into the **manufacturing specification**. Meeting the requirements of **HACCP** (Hazard Analysis and Critical Control Points) is an essential part of quality control, and is discussed in Section 5.

Quality Assurance

While quality control ensures that a production line is working satisfactorily, **quality assurance** refers to all aspects of the processes and procedures going on across the factory. Many food companies now refer to 'food control measures' to sum up the whole area of quality assurance and control. Quality assurance provides a **guarantee** to consumers that all its products are of a certain standard.

Written Question

Spend about 8 minutes answering the following question. You will need some paper and something to write with.

i) What is meant by the term quality control?
(2 marks)

ii) Suggest and outline three occasions on the batch production line for chocolate biscuits where quality control checks could be carried out. *(6 marks)*

Topic 4 Study Guide 5 — Industrial Food Product Design (2)

Here's what you need to know...

about identifying HACCP procedures.

See *Design & Make It! Food Technology* Revised pages 134–137 (127–129 earlier edition).

KEYWORDS

Do you know what the following terms mean?
- HACCP
- Risk factors
- Critical control points

WWW.
Go to:
www.foodstandards.gov.uk/foodindustry/haccp/
www.bmesonline.org.uk
(click on Interactives, then Cyburgers)
www.foodforum.org.uk/ffiles/
(select Focus on HACCP)

What is HACCP?

HACCP stands for Hazard Analysis and Critical Control Points. HACCP is a system concerned with the safety of a food product. It is an extremely important part of planning the processing of food products as it helps to ensure that they are completely safe to eat.

Hazards can be biological, physical or chemical. They can occur at any stage in production, from the preparation of raw ingredients to the distribution to the retailer and consumer.

Assessing the Risk

HACCP relies on the identification of **risk factors** before, during and after production. Possible hazards at each stage of production need to be clearly identified. For example, in the production of bread dough:

- fragments of metal could come away from the stirring paddles of a mixer.
- a hairnet could fall into the mixer.
- the temperature in the tunnel ovens could be set too low.

These **risks** are then analysed:

- How likely are they to happen?
- How serious are the consequences to the safety and quality of the product?

Critical Control Points

A few hazards may be considered to be extremely unlikely to happen and of no consequence to the safety and quality of the product. For all the rest, preventative measures and regular testing and checking procedures must be planned. Each such hazard is known as a **critical control point**. In terms of food safety, the control of temperatures and times are generally considered the most important.

Many critical control points can be effectively monitored, logged and controlled using **ICT**.

Critical Control Points
22. Check for microbiological survival
28. Check for cross-contamination
31. Check for cleanliness
35. Check for microbiological growth
39. Check for physical contamination

Written Question

Spend about 12 minutes answering the following question. You will need some paper and something to write with.

i) Explain what is meant by high-risk food ingredients. *(4 marks)*
ii) Discuss the control methods for high-risk ingredients that might be used in a HACCP. *(8 marks)*

Topic 5 Study Guide 1 — **Food Production Systems**

Input, Process and Output Activities

A food production system is made up of an organised series of activities that work together. There are **three** main parts:

Input: the raw materials, machinery and workforce that go into the system, e.g. wheatgrains, heat.

Process: the activities that take place to change the input into the output, e.g. milling, baking. A fuller definition would be 'a number of activities, in a particular order, that result in changes to the input to produce the final product'.

Output: the finished products, e.g. loaves of bread, and any **waste by-products** that may be produced during manufacture, e.g. bran.

Here's what you need to know...

about how input, process and output activities work together to make up a food production system.

See *Design & Make It! Food Technology* Revised page 121 (113 earlier edition).

KEYWORDS
Do you know what the following terms mean?
- Input
- Process
- Output
- Sub-system
- Feedback

WWW.
Go to:
www.foodforum.org.uk

Sub-systems

Some systems are **complex** and may be divided into several smaller **sub-systems** so that they can be more easily controlled. For example, fruit pies may have a system in place for the pastry production and a different system for the filling.

Some sub-system processing may take place away from the main production line or even by another manufacturing company.

The various sub-systems come together for the final **assembly**.

Feedback

Successful production systems also include **feedback** on each of these activities. This is a series of built in checks that enable the **quality** of the production system to be monitored. As a result, any faults in the system can be corrected immediately and product quality is not put at risk.

Successful Systems

A good production system prevents unnecessary **wastage** of time and resources and reduces the number of unsatisfactory products. This saves money for the manufacturer.

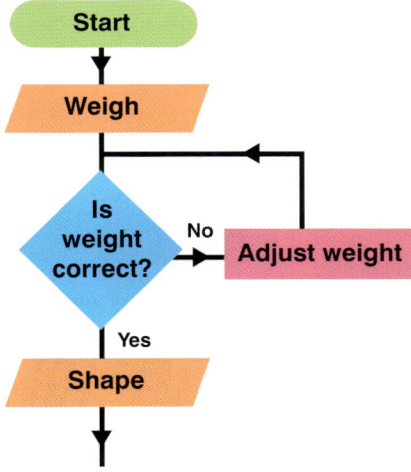

Written Question

Spend about 6 minutes answering the following question. You will need some paper and something to write with.

In a food production system, what is meant by the terms input, process and output? Give an example of each. *(6 marks)*

Topic 5 Study Guide 2 — Food Production Systems

Here's what you need to know...

about how CAD is used to design products and simulate manufacturing systems.

See *Design & Make It! Food Technology* Revised pages 13, 122–123 (114–115 earlier edition).

KEYWORDS
Do you know what the following terms mean?
- Computer Aided Design (CAD)
- Manufacturing simulation

WWW.
Go to:
www.foodtech.org.uk

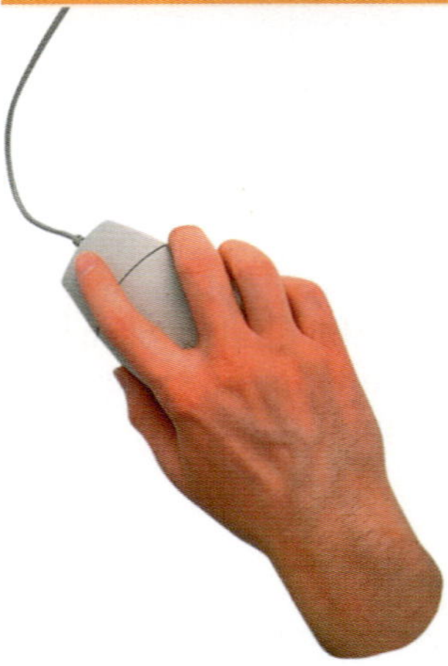

Computer Aided Design

Designing a new food product with the aid of a computer is known as **Computer Aided Design**, or **CAD**. CAD means that a manufacturer can get a good idea of what a new product will be like and be able to test the production process without actually making it in any quantity. This is known as **manufacturing simulation**

CAD can be used to:

- calculate the **nutritional value** of the food product.
- work out the sizes and costs of different **batch** production runs.
- work out the shelf-life of a product.
- present the product's **sensory profile**.
- predict what may happen if ingredients or methods are changed.
- plan how the product will be manufactured.
- check that a **HACCP** (Hazard Analysis and Critical Control Points) procedure will work efficiently.
- present ideas for the packaging.

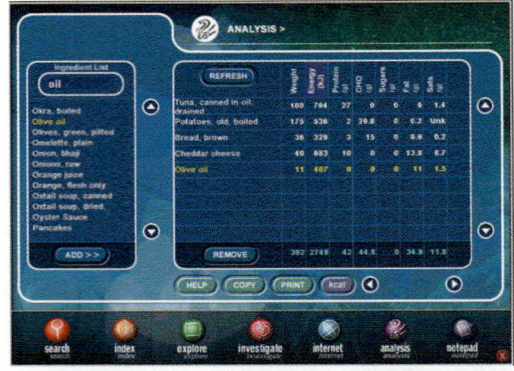

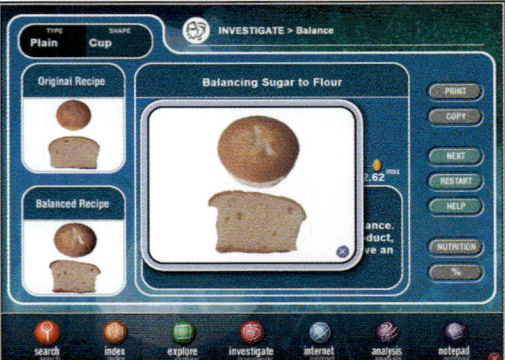

Advantages of CAD
- Saves time: different ideas can be easily and quickly tried out before setting up production.
- Saves costs: costs for **scaling up** product can be predicted and modified if not considered value for money.
- Production **simulation** can avoid the expense of buying unnecessary equipment or workers.
- Avoids human error in testing ideas and calculations.

Disadvantages of CAD
- Results in a loss of jobs as computers take over some of the work.
- There is a shortage of skilled computer operatives in the industry.
- It is expensive to set up.

Written Question

Spend about 4 minutes answering the following question. You will need some paper and something to write with.

Describe one way in which using CAD to simulate manufacture can help to save actual production costs.

(4 marks)

Topic 5 Study Guide 3   **Food Production Systems**

Computer Aided manufacture (CAM)

Here's what you need to know...

about the use of Computer Aided Manufacture (CAM) in food production systems.

See *Design & Make It! Food Technology* Revised page 13 (not featured in earlier edition).

KEYWORDS

Do you know what the following terms mean?
- Computer Aided manufacture (CAM)
- Automated manufacture
- Data logging
- Designated tolerance

WWW.
Go to:
www.foodtech.org.uk

CAM is often carried out as part of **automated manufacture**; using computers to control pre-programmed equipment to make products. This includes **monitoring** and **controlling** production.

For example, a machine can be programmed to add different amounts of various ingredients into a mixture, and then mix them together for exactly the right amount of time. CAM can also be used to monitor and control the temperature of the mixture.

Uses of CAM

There are many uses for CAM in the food industry.

- Automated production processes.
- **Data logging**, e.g. recording **pH values**, temperatures.
- Responding to monitoring **feedback**, e.g. reducing or increasing temperature of environment as needed.
- Control of **designated tolerances**, e.g. weight, dimensions, moisture content, flavour, colour, shape.

Advantages of CAM
- Saves time: more products made, continuous production.
- Continual monitoring: **consistent**, precise products.
- Reliability: less chance of human error when monitoring critical control points.
- Increases productivity: better value for money.
- Safer for workers: reduces personal risk from hazardous tasks.
- Can deal efficiently with large amounts of data.

Disadvantages of CAM
- Results in a loss of jobs as computers take over some of the work.
- Requires skilled computer operators to set up and run: these operators are in short supply in food manufacturing.
- It is expensive to set up the initial production system.

Written Question

Spend about 6 minutes answering the following question. You will need some paper and something to write with.

Explain three advantages to be gained by a manufacturer using computers to aid manufacture.

(6 marks)

Topic 5 Study Guide 4 | Food Production Systems

Making Sense of it All

Electronic **sensors** are used to send information about a machine or device to a computer system. If the data falls outside **acceptable limits** the computer sends a signal to the machine to change, or **control**, the way it is operating. This helps ensure that the products turn out exactly as intended. Sensor and control systems form an important part of the **CAM** (**Computer Aided Manufacture**) process.

Sensors

Sensors may take the form of:

- thermostats, to detect and maintain the temperature.
- thermometers, to detect the temperature.
- food probes, to detect the inner temperature of food.
- light detectors, to detect the thickness of foods by measuring the amount of light passing through.
- metal detectors, to detect any metal fragments in the food.
- light refractors, to detect the density and colour of foods.

Sensors may be used to control:

- moisture content, e.g. checks on products that may dry out during storage.
- temperature, e.g. cooking, storing, chilling, freezing, baking.
- colour **tolerance** of final product, e.g. acceptable levels of browning.
- weights, e.g. unit weight of standard components, individual ingredients, final products.
- **pH levels**, e.g. changes that may occur during preparation, cooking, storing.
- bacterial content, e.g. effects of storage, cooking, preparation.
- any hazardous metal that may be in the final product.

Often sensors are attached to alarms that will alert workers should the production system fail to reach the necessary specifications.

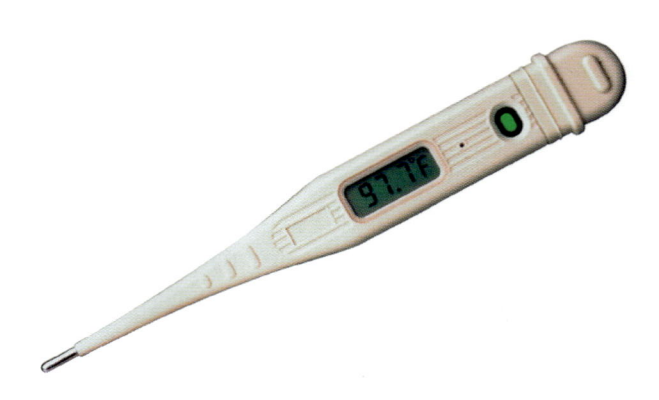

Here's what you need to know...

about the use of sensors and control to maintain quality in food products.

See *Design & Make It! Food Technology* Revised page 13 (not featured in earlier edition).

KEYWORDS

Do you know what the following terms mean?
- Sensor
- Control
- CAM

Written Question

Spend about 8 minutes answering the following question. You will need some paper and something to write with.

Identify four different types of sensors and briefly describe how each may be used in the manufacture of a batch of Swiss rolls.

(8 marks)

Topic 5 Study Guide 5 — Food Production Systems

Here's what you need to know...

about the need for critical points in controlled testing.

See *Design & Make It! Food Technology* Revised pages 134–137 (126–129 earlier edition).

KEYWORDS
Do you know what the following terms mean?
- Critical Control Points
- HACCP
- Risk assessment
- Acceptable levels

WWW.
Go to:
www.foodstandards.gov.uk/foodindustry/haccp/

Critical Control Points

A **critical control point** is any stage in the production system where a food **hazard** can be removed or a safety **risk** can be reduced. This is achieved by **controlled testing**, and is part of the **HACCP** (Hazard Analysis and Critical Control Points) system of **risk assessments** for food safety.

Critical control points refer to:

- temperature
- weight
- time
- food hygiene
- personal hygiene

For example:

- Purchase, e.g. controlling **bacterial content** of raw ingredients.
- Delivery, e.g. control of **shelf-life** of raw materials.
- Storage of materials, e.g. controlling temperature of refrigerator.
- Preparation, e.g. controlling **cross-contamination** from other foods or workers.
- Cooking, e.g. controlled times for cooking to ensure food is safe to eat.
- Finishing, e.g. controlling cooled temperature before adding cream.
- Packaging, e.g. control of risks from **bacterial contamination**.
- Storage of final product, e.g. controlled chilled temperature.

Control

Each critical control point needs to be monitored, either automatically or by a worker. If there is a problem, the planned **corrective action** must immediately be taken to:

- bring the risk back to **acceptable levels** (i.e. the lowest level of risk to a person's health).
- review the production processes involved to help ensure the problem does not happen again.

Written Question

Spend about 10 minutes answering the following question. You will need some paper and something to write with.

A manufacturer needs to ensure that beef burgers made on a production line are not hazardous to the consumer's health. State the hazard and describe the control procedure for each of the five critical control points listed below:

1 Buying ingredients
2 Storage of ingredients
3 Preparation
4 Cooking
5 Packaging

(10 marks)

Topic 6 Study Guide 1 — Packaging and Labelling

Here's what you need to know...

about why food products need to be packaged.

See *Design & Make It! Food Technology* Revised pages 154–155 (146–147 earlier edition).

KEYWORDS
Do you know what the following terms mean?
- Modified atmospheric packaging (MAP)
- Tamperproof packaging

WWW.
Go to:
www.incpen.co.uk
www.j-sainsbury.co.uk/education/tasteofsuccess/secondary.htm

It's in the Bag!

There are a variety of reasons why food sold in supermarkets is packaged. Packaging can protect and preserve the food, inform the consumer about its contents, or it may be a **legal requirement**.

To Protect the Product
The product must be protected from:
- physical damage during transportation.
- chemical **contamination**.
- **micro-organisms**, insects or rodents, and any changes in temperature, light or humidity.

To Contain the Product
The packaging must contain the product for safe transportation, storage and display. Manufacturers specifically design packages to make awkward shaped products easier to handle, stack, store and distribute, e.g. fresh fruit/vegetables.

To Preserve the Product
Packaging can be a part of the **preservation** process, e.g. tinned cans and **modified atmospheric** packaging. Modified atmospheric packaging is a technique that flushes foods with a mixture of gases to prolong their **shelf-life**. Fresh pasta packaged using this technique can keep for up to 3 months in refrigerated conditions. Fresh meat, fish, cheeses and salads will keep for up to 10 days.

To Identify and Provide Information on the Product
Accurate **labelling** is required by law to describe and inform the customer about the product and its contents. This helps customers to choose exactly what they want and make informed choices on food products.

To Prevent Tampering
Tamperproof packaging techniques now make it easy to detect if a package has been opened. Examples include plastic collars on bottle tops, paper strips across jar lids and aluminium foil seals on fruit juice cartons.

Rules and Regulations
Government food **regulations** on food packaging state that packaging must not:
- be hazardous to human health.
- cause the food to **deteriorate**.
- cause unacceptable changes to the actual food or the quality of the food.

Written Question

Spend about 11 minutes answering the following question. You will need some paper and something to write with.

Almost all of the food we buy today is packaged.

i) List five reasons why food is packaged. *(5 marks)*
ii) Discuss three advantages of food packaging for the customer. *(6 marks)*

Topic 6 Study Guide 2 — Packaging and Labelling

Here's what you need to know...

about the main materials used in food packaging.

See *Design & Make It! Food Technology* Revised pages 156–157 (148–149 earlier edition).

KEYWORDS
Do you know what the following term means?
- Packaging materials

WWW.
Go to:
www.incpen.co.uk
www.cannedfood.co.uk

Packing It In

There are four main materials used in food packaging today:

- Glass
- Metal
- Plastics
- Paper and card

Each material has its own individual **properties** and **uses**.

Glass

Drinks, jams, chutneys, pickles, sauces, herbs/spices are all contained in glass bottles or jars. Glass is:
- easy to mould
- rigid
- **impermeable**
- economical
- attractive
- strong
- fragile
- recyclable
- heavy
- **non-reactive** with the foods inside
- available in clear or coloured varieties

Plastics

Wrappers over fresh products (e.g. bread, yoghurt and salad pots), bags for cereals, salads, fruits and vegetables, soft drink bottles are made from a variety of different types of plastics. Plastic is:
- easy to mould into shape
- lightweight
- easy to fold and print on
- easy to **fuse** to seal

Special **heat resistant plastics** are used for **cook-chill** products.

Metals

Tinned products (e.g. beans, tuna), aluminium cans for soft drinks and screw tops on bottles are made from different types of metals. Metal is:
- strong
- impermeable
- able to withstand heat treatments
- easy to mould
- lightweight
- recyclable

Paper and Card

Labels, bags, boxes, wrappers and packets are all made from various types of paper and card. As well as thickness, the **finish** applied makes a great deal of difference to the material's properties. Paper and card are:
- easy to print on
- easy to coat, wax or treat
- recyclable
- lightweight
- easy to fold and mould
- flexible
- **permeable**

Mixed Materials

The majority of food packaging is a combination of two or more materials, e.g. mayonnaise may be packaged in a glass bottle with a metal lid, paper label and a plastic **tamperproof** seal.

Written Question

Spend about 9 minutes answering the following question. You will need some paper and something to write with.

Lasagne is a popular 'cook-chill' convenience product.

i) Name three suitable materials that could be used for the packaging. *(3 marks)*

ii) Give reasons for your choice of each material. *(6 marks)*

Topic 6 Study Guide 3 — Packaging and Labelling

Here's what you need to know...

about writing specifications for food packaging.

See *Design & Make It! Food Technology* Revised pages 158–159 (150–151 earlier edition).

KEYWORDS
Do you know what the following terms mean?
- Shelf-life
- Modified atmospheric packaging (MAP)
- Food packaging specification

www.
Go to:
www.incpen.co.uk

Getting the Packaging Right

A food manufacturer must carefully match the food product with the most **suitable** form of packaging. For example, fresh salmon steaks are a high risk, oxygen sensitive and fairly delicate food. They require refrigeration to extend their **shelf-life** and reduce **micro-orgamism** activity. Therefore the packaging needs to:

- provide protection.
- stop air (oxygen) getting in.
- possibly use **modified atmospheric packaging (MAP)** to prolong its shelf-life and be suitable for chilled storage.

A suitable solution would be a plastic tray with a heat sealed barrier covering with or without MAP.

Writing a Specification

The checklist below highlights important criteria for a **food packaging specification**.

The packaging must:

- be **compatible** with the food and not affect its flavour.
- be fit for its intended usage (e.g. **cook-chill**, microwave).
- conform to labelling **legislation**.
- be able to have labelling information printed on to it.
- be **cost effective**.

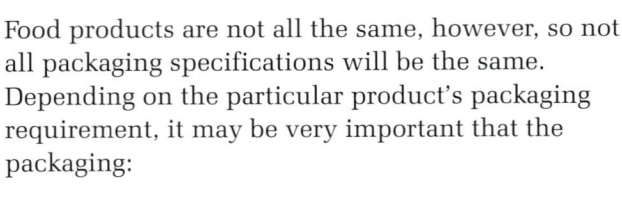

Food products are not all the same, however, so not all packaging specifications will be the same. Depending on the particular product's packaging requirement, it may be very important that the packaging:

- is airtight, to prevent dehydration/weight loss.
- provides a moisture barrier, to prevent or slow down micro-orgamisms.
- is firmly sealed.
- is strong enough to protect the product during delivery and storage.
- doesn't get altered by changes in temperature – e.g. **heat resistant** plastics for when food is cooked in its packaging.
- is attractive so that consumers want to buy the product.
- allows the customer to see the product inside.

Written Question

Spend about 10 minutes answering the following question. You will need some paper and something to write with.

Write a possible specification for the packaging of a tuna salad sandwich.

(10 marks)

Topic 6 Study Guide 4 — Packaging and Labelling

Here's what you need to know...

about about the labelling of food products.

See *Design & Make It! Food Technology* Revised pages 162–165 (154–157 earlier edition).

KEYWORDS
Do you know what the following terms mean?
- Barcodes
- Batch lots
- Nutritional information
- Environmental issues
- Genetic modification

WWW.
Go to:
www.beakman.com/upc/barcode.html
www.dotprint.com/fgen/barcodes.htm
www.foodstandards.gov.uk/foodindustry/

Looking at the Label

Food labels and packages contain essential information to help customers make **informed choices** about food products and compare similar products.

The **1996 Food Labelling Regulations** state that a food label must include all the following essential information:

❶ *The name of the product.* This must be clearly displayed informing the customer exactly what is in the product, e.g. chicken drumsticks, chocolate chip cookies.

❷ *The contact details of the manufacturer* – the name and address of the manufacturer.

❸ *A list of all ingredients* – in descending order of weight (largest to smallest). All **additives** must also be listed.

❹ *Storage instructions*, giving specific details of the best conditions and temperatures for safe storage.

❺ The **shelf-life** of the product must be shown specifying either the Use by or Sell by date of the product.

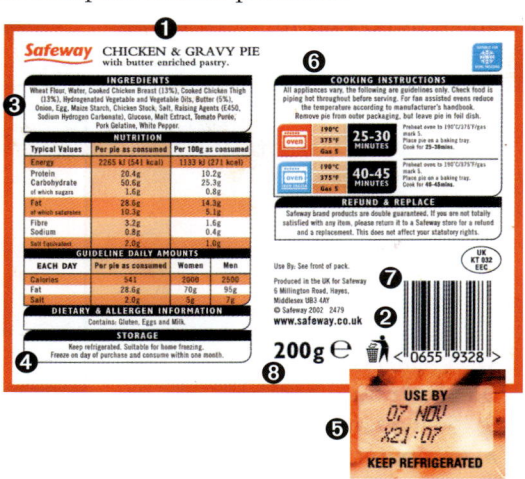

❻ *Cooking instructions* (how to prepare the product) if appropriate.

❼ *The country from where the product originated.*

❽ *The net weight of the product with a large **e** to highlight that this is an average quantity.*

Manufacturers may also choose to include the following information:

Batch lots recording dates of production, production lines and packaging details.

Special or **nutritional information** about the product, e.g. suitable for vegetarians, freezing, microwaving or not suitable for nut allergy sufferers.

Special information on **environmental issues** that might relate to the product or packaging, e.g. made from recyclable materials or non-**genetically modified (GM)**

Barcodes to provide quicker/more efficient checkout service and itemised bill receipts.

Written Question

Spend about 10 minutes answering the following question. You will need some paper and something to write with.

i) Most food packaging now has a barcode. List the advantages of a barcode on a food label to:
   a) the consumer   b) the retailer   *(4 marks)*

ii) The label on some sweet and sour chicken states: Display until 9 April/Use by 10 April. Why does the government make food manufacturers put a 'use by' date on food packages like this one?   *(2 marks)*

iii) The cooking instructions on a packet of prawn spring rolls are as follows:

From chilled:
1. Pre heat the oven to 200°C, 400°F, Gas mark 6.
2. Remove all packaging.
3. Place spring rolls on a wire rack on a baking tray in the middle of the oven and cook for 15 minutes.

Always check that the product is piping hot and the pastry is crispy.
All cooking appliances vary, these are guidelines only.

Why is it important that manufacturers print accurate cooking and defrosting instructions on packages of products such as prawn spring rolls?   *(4 marks)*

Topic 6 Study Guide 5 | Packaging and Labelling

Here's what you need to know...

about using CAD to design packaging information.

See *Design & Make It! Food Technology* Revised pages 13, 34–35 and 165 (26–27 and 157 earlier edition).

KEYWORDS
Do you know what the following terms mean?
- Computer Aided Design (CAD)
- Nutritional information
- Computer Aided Manufacture (CAM)

Using CAD

When producing packaging or labels for food products, **Computer Aided Design** can be used to:

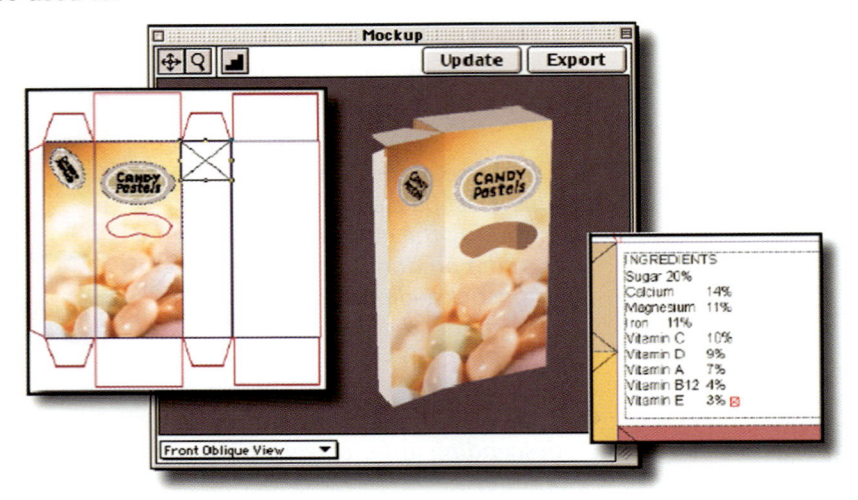

- Design parts of the package/label, e.g. **net**, pictures, text.
- Automatically produce **barcodes**.
- Position digital photographs of food products on the package design.
- Experiment with **font** and colour combinations on the package.

Nutritional Information

More manufacturers are now putting **nutritional information** on their food packages. This is because consumers have an increasing awareness of healthy eating and food allergies.

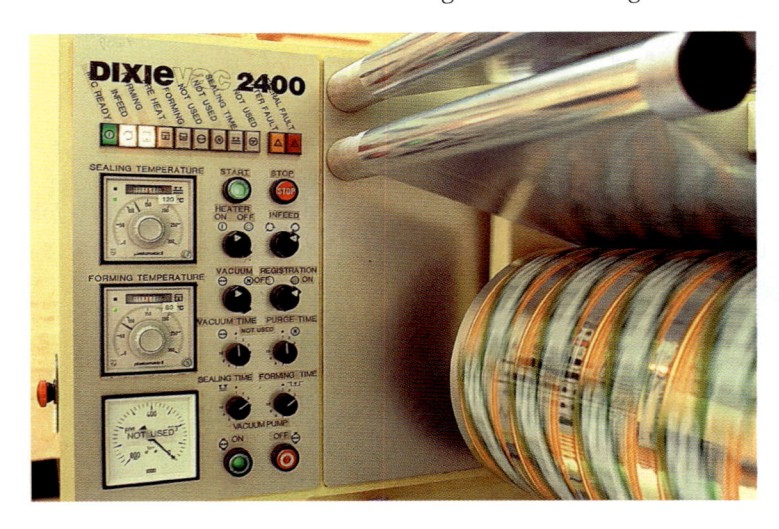

Computers can be used to carry out detailed **analysis** of food products. Special **nutritional analysis** software is available that automatically generates nutritional information that can be copied directly into a graphics program used in the design of the label.

Using CAM

During the manufacture of a package, **Computer Aided Manufacture** can be used to control processes such as the cutting of the packaging net, the printing, the temperatures of plastic or wax coatings, glue, etc.

Written Question

Spend about 4 minutes answering the following question. You will need some paper and something to write with.

Explain two different ways in which Computer Aided Design could be used to design a food label. *(4 marks)*

Topic 6 Study Guide 6 | Packaging and Labelling

Here's what you need to know...

about nutritional information on food packaging.

See *Design & Make It! Food Technology* Revised pages 13, 34–35, 164–165 (26–27, 156–157 earlier edition).

KEYWORDS
Do you know what the following term means?
- Nutritional information

Nutritional Information

Including **nutritional information** on food packaging is **voluntary**. However, the Government has recommended that if manufacturers do put nutritional information on their packaging, they should list the product's ingredients, nutrients and energy in a **standard** way. This will ensure it doesn't take people too long to work out what the information is saying.

Special Claims

When a manufacturer makes a special claim about a food, e.g. reduced fat, low salt, low sugar, high fibre, the **Food Labelling Regulations of 1996** lay down strict criteria that must be followed:

- To be described as **low in fat** a product, e.g. a yoghurt, must have a total fat content of 5 grams or less per serving of 100g/100mls or above.
- To be described as **low in sugar** the total sugar content must be less than 5 grams per portion of 100g/100mls or above.
- To be described as **reduced fat**, e.g. a reduced fat dessert, the total fat content must be at least 25% less than the original product.
- To be described as a **source of fibre** a product must contain at least 3g per 100g/100ml portion.
- To be described as **rich in fibre** a product, e.g. breakfast cereal, must contain at least 6 grams of fibre per 100g/100mls portion.

Further Information

Additional information may be given on polyunsaturated fats, starch, cholesterol, vitamins and minerals. **Special dietary claims** may also be printed, e.g. suitable for vegetarians, gluten free, no added colour or this product may contain traces of nuts.

Written Question

Spend about 12 minutes answering the following question. You will need some paper and something to write with.

a) What are advantages of putting nutritional information about a food product on the package? *(3 marks)*

b) The information on the right shows part of a label for some coleslaw.
   i) How much energy will a 50g portion of this coleslaw provide? *(1 mark)*
   ii) Name the two main ingredients in mayonnaise. *(2 marks)*
   iii) State two ways this basic coleslaw recipe could be changed to make the product healthier. Explain how each change will make the product promote healthy eating. *(4 marks)*
   iv) The coleslaw contains stabilisers. Why are stabilisers added to the coleslaw? *(2 marks)*

INGREDIENTS

Cabbage (53%), Mayonnaise (34%), (Vegetable oil; Vinegar; Water; Sugar; Pasteurised egg yolk; Salt; Dijon mustard; Stabilisers: Guar Gum; Xanthan Gum), Carrot (12%), Onion (1%).

Nutritional information

TYPICAL COMPOSITION	100g (3oz) provide
ENERGY	654KJ/158 Kcal
PROTEIN	2.2 g
CARBOHYDRATES	5.2 g
of which are sugars	5.2 g
FAT	14.3g
of which are saturates	1.1 g
FIBRE	1.6 g
SODIUM	0.4 g

Topic 7 Study Guide 1 — Social and Economic Implications

Here's what you need to know...

about social, moral, cultural, economic and environmental issues in food technology.

See *Design & Make It! Food Technology* Revised pages 34–35, 100–101, 146–147, 160 (26–27, 92–93, 138–139, 152 earlier edition).

KEYWORDS
Do you know what the following terms mean?
- Health issues
- Social issues
- Cultural issues
- Moral issues
- Environmental issues
- Economic issues

WWW.
Go to:
www.nutrition.org.uk
www.littleredtractor.org.uk

Health Issues
In food technology, **health issues** can arise when a food product has an unforeseen effect on a group of people. In the 1990s, the **BSE crisis** (when beef products were linked with human brain disease) meant that many people stopped buying beef and sales of **non-meat protein** foods, like Quorn, soya and tofu, increased.

Social Issues
Social issues arise in food technology when a new product has an impact on the way some people live their lives. For example, 'convenience' foods mean both parents can go out to full-time work, but result in fewer families sitting down to eat together.

Cultural Issues
Food is a very important part of life and some foods or ingredients have special meanings. In Jewish culture, for example, religious people do not eat certain foods. Therefore, food technology needs to take **cultural issues** into account or products may end up not being bought by **target markets**.

Moral Issues
What people think of as right and wrong is an important part of what makes up a society or culture. If something is morally wrong, we mean it's wrong because it goes against what we believe. A food product might make business sense, or seem fine to a lot of people, but there would still be a **moral issue** if it went against people's beliefs or values.

For example, some people think it is morally wrong for food products to be **genetically modified**. They believe that this process is unnatural. A lot of people also think it is unethical (morally wrong) for Western companies to buy products such as coffee, cocoa or tea very cheaply from poor countries and then sell them in the West for much higher prices, keeping all the profit for themselves. Fair Trade products are now available in many shops and guarantee a better deal for Third World producers

Environmental Issues
Environmental issues arise as we become more conscious of the effect we have on our planet. In today's 'throw away' society, where one third of all rubbish is packaging, designers must consider ways to minimise the amount of packaging a food product has and limit its impact on the environment.

Not so long ago most of the food we ate was produced locally. Today, transporting food products over long distances uses up valuable oil resources and **pollutes** the atmosphere.

Economic Issues
Economic issues are to do with the price and cost of food products. For example, imported food is often cheaper than food grown or reared in this country – often because it costs a lot less to produce food in countries where farm labour is very cheap, or where governments give farmers money to keep prices low.

Economic issues can often come into conflict with social and moral issues: for example, battery farming of hens is a very good way of producing a lot of cheap eggs, but some people think it is cruel to the hens and, therefore, morally wrong.

Written Question

Spend about 8 minutes answering the following question. You will need some paper and something to write with.

i) Identify a basic food product that is regularly purchased (e.g. coffee, tea, chocolate, fruit or vegetables). Outline the social and economic issues that the manufacturer or retailer might have addressed. *(4 marks)*

ii) Discuss a specific situation where a food manufacturer or retailer has had to consider environmental issues. *(4 marks)*

Topic 7 Study Guide 2 — Social and Economic Implications

Here's what you need to know...

about healthy eating food products.

See *Design & Make It! Food Technology* Revised pages 80–83, 146–149 (72–75, 138–141 earlier edition).

KEYWORDS
Do you know what the following terms mean?
- Non starch polysaccharide (NSP)
- Recipe engineering
- Alternative ingredients

WWW.
Go to:
www.nutrition.org.uk
www.foodstandards.gov.uk
www.meatmatters.com/health

The Health of the Nation

We live in a society of plenty with a vast choice of foods, often combining greater quality with good value. However, we are now becoming increasingly concerned about the consequences and possible side effects of this on our health. In 1998, the government published *Saving Lives: Our Healthier Nation*. This outlined ways in which **diet-related diseases** could be reduced or avoided. It claims that, as a nation, we need to improve our diet by:

- eating less fat, especially **saturated fat**.
- eating more foods rich in fibre and **non starch polysaccharide (NSP)**.
- eating less salt and highly processed foods.
- eating less sugar.

The food industry has responded to these **healthy eating** issues in many ways. Some of their solutions are listed below.

Less is More

The development of low fat, low sugar, low salt and high fibre versions of many foods, e.g. Sainsbury's 'Be Good To Yourself' range.

Recipe Engineering

Recipe engineering to improve the **nutritional profile** of a product, e.g. some margarines now contain Omega 3 because the fatty acids from oily fish are believed to reduce the risk of heart disease.

Different Dietary Needs

The development of a range of products to cater for a wide variety of dietary needs, e.g. **alternative ingredients** including **TVP**, **Quorn** and **Tofu** to meet the needs of the vegetarian consumer or a range of **gluten free** foods for **coeliacs**.

Information

The use of clear, accurate and full information on packaging allows customers to make **informed choices** and compare similar products.

Many retailers now have customer service departments, web sites, in-store magazines, and customer leaflets providing information about products and other food related issues.

Written Question

Spend about 4 minutes answering the following question. You will need some paper and something to write with.

Food manufacturers now produce many more products that help healthy eating.

Give two ways in which manufacturers can adapt existing recipes to meet the demand for healthier options.

(4 marks)

Topic 7 Study Guide 3 — **Social and Economic Implications**

Here's what you need to know...

about the use of genetically modified and organic foods.

See *Design & Make It! Food Technology* Revised pages 84, 116, 142 (76, 108, 134 earlier edition).

KEYWORDS
Do you know what the following term means?
- Genetically modified (GM) food

WWW.
Go to:
www.organicfood.co.uk
www.foodfuture.org.uk

Genetically Modified Food

Genetic modification or **genetic engineering** is used to change the characteristics and qualities of certain foods. Scientists identify and engineer a **gene** that makes up a characteristic in a food. Individual genes can be copied and transferred between plants and animals to improve flavour, **nutritional value**, colour, size, **shelf-life** and other desirable qualities. There are many potential advantages and disadvantages of using **genetically modified foods**.

Advantages of GM foods
- **GM foods** make food crops more resistant to pests and disease.
- GM foods improve the quality and **nutritional value** of a product.
- There is a saving in energy for producers.
- The ripening process in fruit and vegetables can be slowed down.
- Possible modifications can be made to food products to prevent life threatening reactions, e.g. peanuts.
- Wheat can be modified to be gluten free.
- Crop yields can be increased and the amount of food obtained from animals.
- Fewer pesticides need to be used on GM crops that have been made pest and disease resistant.

Disadvantages of GM foods
- There are safety concerns because the long-term effects on health are not yet known.
- Genes could escape and transfer to another species with unwanted consequences.
- The increase in **herbicides** causes harm to plants, insects and birds.
- There would be a loss of trade for developing countries.

Organic Foods

Many people today are more concerned than they used to be about food quality, the way animals are treated and what we are doing to the environment. This has meant that **organic food** products are becoming more and more popular. Organic food is food grown, reared and manufactured in as 'natural' a way as possible, with the minimum of artificial chemicals and processes.

There are a range of advantages and disadvantages associated with organic foods.

Advantages of organic foods
- The absence of chemicals, hormones and **antibiotics** make products safer to eat, and for farmers to work with.
- Organic foods are free from harmful **additives** that often cause food allergies.
- Organic foods do not use GM or **irradiated** products.
- Organic foods are high quality products that often taste better
- The natural fertility of the soil improves.
- There is less chemical pollution of rivers.
- Bees, butterflies, birds and wildlife are no longer poisoned by pesticides.
- Animals benefit by being in less **intensive** surroundings.

Disadvantages of organic foods
- Organic foods are often more expensive to buy due to production methods.
- Organic foods are not available in all shops.
- The **product range** is more limited.
- It is expensive and risky for farmers to re-equip farms to convert to organic methods.

Written Question

Spend about 10 minutes answering the following question. You will need some paper and something to write with.

Consumers are becoming increasingly concerned about the use of genetically modified foods. Discuss the advantages and disadvantages of genetically modifying food products.

(10 marks)

Topic 7 Study Guide 4 — Social and Economic Implications

About Additives

Here's what you need to know...

about the advantages and disadvantages of using additives.

See *Design & Make It! Food Technology* Revised pages 72, 97, 100–101 (64, 89 earlier edition).

KEYWORDS
Do you know what the following term means?
- Additives

WWW.
Go to:
www.faia.org.uk
www.ifst.org

Additives are **synthetic** or natural substances added to food during processing. Additives can extend the **shelf life**, improve the flavour and appearance, and maintain or increase the **nutritional value** of a product. There is further coverage of the use of food additives in Topic 8 Section 5.

Government and European Community controls state that no additives that have been proved dangerous are allowed in foods. The use of additives is strictly controlled by law and additives must be listed on all food labels. However, some consumers have decided to avoid some common additives because they believe they have unwelcome **side effects** on health. These consumers tend to be interested in more 'natural' food products.

The advantages of additives
- Provide a wide range of products to meet the consumer's needs.
- Help the processing and preparation of foods.
- Prevent food **spoilage** and extend the **shelf life** of a product.
- Improve or enhance the colour, flavour and appearance of a product.
- Maintain or improve the **nutritional value** of a product.
- Help produce a **consistent** product on a large scale, e.g. mayonnaise.

The disadvantages of additives
- A number of people may be sensitive or allergic to additives and suffer side effects, e.g. asthma, rashes, hyperactivity.
- Although additives are tested, it is not always possible to forecast the long-term effects they have on our health.
- They can be used to disguise poor quality ingredients.
- Some colours and flavours are often unnecessary.

REDUCED CALORIE MAYONNAISE
INGREDIENTS: Water, Vegetable Oil (30%), Fructose-Glucose Syrup, Modified Maize Starch, Pasteurised Egg Yolk (4.5%), Spirit Vinegar, Salt, Acidity Regulators (Lactic Acid, Sodium Lactate), Preservative (Potassium Sorbate), Stabiliser (Xanthan Gum), Flavouring, Lemon Juice.
WARNING: This product may contain traces of nuts, as it has been made in a factory that uses nut ingredients.
Suitable for Vegetarians
STORE IN A COOL, DRY PLACE
RECYCLABLE GLASS

Written Question

Answer the following question on plain or lined paper. Do not spend more than 8 minutes writing your answer.

Look carefully at the label below. It has been taken from an instant hot chocolate drink.

i) Identify the two additives present in the chocolate drink. *(4 marks)*

ii) Many food products contain colourings. What are the advantages and disadvantages of using colourings in food? *(4 marks)*

INGREDIENTS

Drinking chocolate, Dried whey, Sugar, Hydrogenated vegetable oil, Dried glucose syrup, Milk chocolate, Dried skimmed milk, Salt, Flavourings, Stabiliser (E399), Emulsifier (E461).

Topic 7 Study Guide 5 — Social and Economic Implications

Find a Bin to Put it In

Today, we live in a throw away society of fast food, take-aways, eating on the move, convenience foods, snacks and drinks. One third of all rubbish is packaging and at the end of the day most packages are simply thrown away. All this is causing **environmental problems**.

Problems with Packaging

Some of the main environmental problems with packaging are:

- the extensive felling of trees to produce the paper and card. This uses valuable resources and can damage **ecosystems**.
- the use of chemicals in the manufacture of plastics can cause air, land and water pollution and damage to natural habitats. It also causes the destruction of the **ozone layer**.
- many products are excessively packaged and this increases litter problems.
- many packaging materials are not **biodegradable** and will not rot away in **landfill sites**.
- landfill sites can build up levels of methane gas and present problems for local. residents. When **incinerated** many plastics give off harmful toxic fumes.

Environmentally Friendly Packaging Solutions

Manufacturers, retailers and consumers all have a part to play in solving the problems with packaging.

Here's what you need to know...

about the effect food packaging has on our environment.

See *Design & Make It! Food Technology* Revised pages 160–161 (152–153 earlier edition).

KEYWORDS
Do you know what the following terms mean?
- Ecosystem
- Biodegradable
- Environmentally friendly
- Recycled materials

Manufacturer's responsibilities

- Use minimum amount of packaging possible – thinner, but stronger.
- Use recycled materials where possible.
- Make it easier for packaging to be recycled.
- Encourage consumers to recycle by printing logos on labels stating the material it is made from and whether it can be recycled.

Retailer's responsibilities

- Encourage manufacturers to use recycled materials and use less packaging.
- Encourage customers to recycle by providing recycling bins near shops.
- Develop biodegradable packaging, e.g. Sainsbury's biodegradable fruit and vegetable packaging.
- Provide information about the importance of recycling.

Consumer's responsibilities

- Recycle as much packaging and as many carrier bags as possible.
- Reuse packaging for other purposes.
- Buy large packs that use less packaging – avoid individually packaged products.
- Choose products that have packaging made from recycled or biodegradable materials.
- Look for the logos on products that tell you if the package can be recycled.
- Pressurise retailers and government to set **legislation** for minimum standards of packaging.

Written Question

Answer the following question on plain or lined paper. Spend about 8 minutes writing your answer.

Many people are concerned about our environment. Discuss ways manufacturers and retailers can become more environmentally aware and reduce waste from food packaging.

(8 marks)

Topic 8 Study Guide 1 | **Combining Ingredients**

Food Product Development

When manufacturers are developing a new product, a **product development team** put together a **prototype**. This follows the **product specification** that came out of all the work the company has done already on researching, formulating and refining their ideas.

When the team has designed the prototype for their new idea they then have to scale up the recipe for **large-scale production**. **Designated tolerances** are set and decisions are made on the use of **standard components** and **additives**.

The development team must make sure that the product retains the same qualities when produced in very large numbers. This often involves adapting the original recipe and adding extra ingredients.

Adapting the Recipe

Recipes can be adapted to:

- alter the **nutritional value**, e.g. low fat yoghurt, vitamin enriched breakfast cereal.
- produce a luxury or lower cost version of the product, e.g. economy sausages.
- make it suitable for specific **target groups**, e.g. vegetarian cakes using no animal products, gluten free biscuits.
- extend a **product range**, e.g. add other flavours to a range of crisps.

Extra Ingredients

The **ratio** of ingredients must remain the same, but some extra ingredients may be added or changed for particular purposes. For example:

- an oil is often used in place of margarine or lard in pastry or biscuits to increase their **plasticity**.
- dextrose is added to baked products to give an improved golden colour when cooked.
- glycerine can be added to increase the moisture of cake mixtures.
- water may be added to create steam, which acts as an extra **raising agent**.
- **additives** are included for specific purposes, e.g. preservatives, colours, etc.

Production Method

Making the product in the factory will be different from making it on a small scale in the test kitchen. Some production methods may need to be changed.

The stages in production have to be in the most efficient order for a production line. **Large-scale**, specialist equipment will need to be used at all stages to reduce **production costs**, reduce the number of workers, and increase **output**.

Here's what you need to know...

about how manufacturers develop recipes for large-scale production.

See *Design & Make It! Food Technology* Revised pages 72–73 (64–65 earlier edition).

KEYWORDS

Do you know what the following terms mean?
- Product development team
- Large-scale production

Written Question

Spend about 8 minutes answering the following question. You will need some paper and something to write with.

A food product development team has designed a small-scale recipe for a new biscuit. For mass production the recipe has to be scaled up and other ingredients added. Explain clearly why each of the following ingredients may be used in the large-scale recipe.

1. Hydrogenated vegetable oil in place of margarine
2. Dextrose
3. Preservatives
4. Flavouring *(8 marks)*

Topic 8 Study Guide 2 — Combining Ingredients

Here's what you need to know...

about the different types of structures found in processed foods.

See *Design & Make It! Food Technology* Revised pages 126–127 (118–119 earlier edition).

KEYWORDS
Do you know what the following terms mean?
- Colloidal structures
- Emulsions
- Foams
- Gels
- Suspensions

WWW.
Go to:
www.foodtech.org.uk

Colloidal Structures

When ingredients are combined a structure is formed which is known as a **colloidal structure**. A colloidal structure has two parts evenly mixed together. The parts could be liquid, solid, or gas.

- A mixture of oil and water is called an **emulsion**.
- A mixture of gas and liquid is called a **foam**.
- A mixture of a small amount of a solid in a large amount of a liquid that becomes set is called a **gel**.

Emulsions

A mixture of oil and water is called an emulsion. If left to stand, an emulsion will separate, but if an **emulsifying agent** is added it will be stabilised and remain mixed.

Examples of emulsions are cream, cake mixtures and mayonnaise.
Examples of emulsifying agents are lecithin, found in egg yolks in cake mixtures and glycerol monostearate, added to margarine.

Foams

A mixture of gas and liquid is called a foam. Trapped air increases the volume of the mix. A solid foam is formed if it is cooked.

Examples of foams are ice cream, whipped cream and mousses.
Examples of solid foams are meringue and soufflé.

Gels

Gels consist of a small amount of a solid mixed in a large amount of a liquid that becomes set. When gels set they are usually soft and **elastic**.

Examples of gels are jam, jelly and mousse. Gelatine sets jelly and mousse, and pectin sets jam.

Suspensions

Suspensions are when an **insoluble** solid is held in a liquid. If left to stand, the solid will sink to the bottom. Stirring keeps them evenly mixed.

Examples of suspensions are gravy and white sauce.

Solutions

Solutions are formed when a **soluble** solid is mixed with a liquid. If left to stand, they will not separate.

An example of a solution is an Oxo cube dissolved in water.

Written Question

Spend about 8 minutes answering the following question. You will need some paper and something to write with.

1. Describe what an emulsion is and give two examples. *(4 marks)*
2. Describe what happens when an emulsion is:
   a) shaken vigorously.
   b) left to stand. *(4 marks)*

Topic 8 Study Guide 3 — Combining Ingredients

Making Pastry

The manufacture of pastry products is a good example of how different ingredients, quantities and processing methods can be used. All types of pastry are made from similar ingredients: flour, fat and water. However, by using different **ratios** and methods, different types of pastry with different characteristics can be produced.

There are three main types of pastry: shortcrust, flaky and choux. They vary in their **consistency**, **volume**, **texture** and **flavour**.

Shortcrust Pastry

Shortcrust pastry is used for pies, pasties and flans, etc. It has a short, light, crisp texture and uses half the weight of fat to flour. Plain flour is used as it contains less gluten.

Sifting the flour adds air (**aeration**). Wholemeal flour can be used to add **fibre**. Margarine or butter adds colour and flavour. White fats give a good texture (**shortening**).

Salt improves the flavour. Water binds the ingredients together and egg yolk can be added to give a richer flavour.

Flaky Pastry

Flaky pastry is used for vol-au-vents and sausage rolls, etc. It has a light, layered texture and uses two thirds fat to flour. Strong plain flour with a high **gluten** content is used, which gives the pastry **elasticity**.

A mixture of margarine and lard is often used to give a good flavour and texture. Layers are formed by repeated rolling, folding and by incorporating fat between the layers. Air trapped in the layers makes the pastry rise.

Lemon juice is added to the water to strengthen the gluten.

Choux Pastry

Choux pastry is used for éclairs, profiteroles and cheese aigrettes, etc. It has a light, crisp texture with a hollow centre, which is filled with cream, etc.

One-third fat to strong flour is used, which is quickly mixed into boiling water.

Some **gelatinisation** takes place. Egg is beaten in which helps the pastry to rise. Steam forms inside the mixture to create the hollow centre. Butter or margarine is used for colour and flavour. The mixture is piped or spooned on to a baking sheet – not rolled.

Here's what you need to know...

about how different ingredients are combined during preparation and cooking.

See *Design & Make It! Food Technology* Revised pages 56–59 (48–51 earlier edition).

KEYWORDS
Do you know what the following terms mean?
- Shortcrust pastry
- Flaky pastry
- Choux pastry

Written Question

Spend about 12 minutes answering the following question. You will need some paper and something to write with.

When designing new food products the developers need to be aware of the functions of each ingredient during the manufacturing process. For example, the main ingredients of flaky pastry are flour, fat, salt and water. Explain the function of each of these ingredients.

(12 marks)

Topic 8 Study Guide 4 — Combining Ingredients

Here's what you need to know...

about how manufacturers ensure products are of a consistent quality.

See *Design & Make It! Food Technology* Revised pages 60–61 (52–53 earlier edition).

KEYWORDS

Do you know what the following terms mean?
- Designated tolerances
- Quality control
- Feedback

Industrial Application

Food manufacturers need to ensure that the food products they produce are of **consistent quality**. This involves the taste, shape, size and finish. New products need to be developed to take into account uniformity in production and **quality control procedures**. The reduction of **waste** is also an important consideration.

Designated Tolerances

Manufacturers work within designated tolerances to ensure their products are of a consistent quality. Designated tolerances help ensure consistency of the product by setting acceptable variations of weight, thickness, colour, viscosity, etc.

For example, if a recipe states the use of 100g of an ingredient it might be decided that any weight between 99 and 101g is acceptable to make a consistent enough product. However, 98.9g or 101.1g would be unacceptable.

These **tolerance levels** are determined during the development of a new food product by the development team. They are then included in the **manufacturing specification**, for example, 'weight 100g + or - 5g'.

Some examples of qualities that will be given designated tolerances are the:

- weight of filling in a pie.
- thickness of biscuit dough.
- **viscosity** of a sauce.
- colour of cooked pastry.

Quality Control and Feedback

Quality control is based on the designated tolerances. Products are checked during production, often by **sensors** linked to computers, and any product outside the designated tolerance will be rejected from the system.

Feedback allows faults to be detected, and the machines to be reset if necessary, to ensure that future products are within the acceptable levels. For example, if oven temperatures are too high or too low they will be adjusted accordingly to keep the product within its designated tolerance temperature.

Written Question

Spend about 6 minutes answering the following question. You will need some paper and something to write with.

During the development of a new chicken and vegetable pie the test kitchen has set designated tolerances to be used in large-scale production.

1. Explain the term 'designated tolerances'. *(2 marks)*
2. Give four examples of limits that could be set for these pies. *(4 marks)*

Topic 8 Study Guide 5 — Combining Ingredients

Additives

Additives are **synthetic** or **natural** substances added in small quantities to food during processing for a particular purpose. The advantages and disadvantages of using additives are discussed in Topic 7 Section 4.

Additives are essential in most food processing:

- **Thickening** and **gelling agents** improve the texture of foods, e.g. jam.
- Colourings make the food look more attractive and provide important clues to flavour.
- **Flavourings** and **flavour enhancers** add or improve flavour lost during processing, e.g. herbs and spices, monosodium glutamate.
- **Sweeteners** are used in **low calorie** products in place of sugar, e.g. yoghurts.
- **Anti-caking agents** are used to stop powdered food from sticking together, e.g. salt.

Different Types of Additives

- E100s are colours used to **restore colour** lost during processing, or to improve natural colour, e.g. canned peas.
- E200s are **preservatives** used to keep food safe for eating for longer by stopping the growth of microbes, e.g. bacon, dried fruit.
- E300s are **antioxidants** used to stop food containing fat going rancid, e.g. gravy granules.
- E400s are **emulsifiers** and **stabilisers** used to stop fat and water separating in foods, e.g. salad cream.

Common Additives

The use of additives is strictly controlled by law and additives must be listed on all food labels. Additives must be EC approved and usually start with an E number. Below are some of the more commonly used additives.

Tartrazine is a colouring used in soft drinks and can affect some children and asthmatics.

Monosodium Glutamate (MSG) intensifies the flavours of foods and is widely used in Chinese recipes and savoury products. MSG can cause allergies in some people and can make them feel dizzy and sick.

Xanthan gum is used to thicken salad cream.

Sorbitol is a bulk sweetener, similar to sugar in levels of sweetness and used in sugar free confectionery and some **diabetic products**.

Here's what you need to know...

about the different additives used in the food industry.

See *Design & Make It! Food Technology* Revised pages 100–101 (92–93 earlier edition).

KEYWORDS

Do you know what the following terms mean?
- Additives
- Thickening and gelling agents
- Flavourings and flavour enhancers
- Sweeteners
- Anti-caking agents

WWW.
Go to:
www.faia.org.uk

Written Question

Spend about 10 minutes answering the following question. You will need some paper and something to write with.

Look carefully at the ingredients list of this low calorie dessert mix. Which additives are in this product? Explain why each one has been added. *(10 marks)*

Lemon & Lime Flavour Sugar Free Jelly Crystals made with Sweeteners.

Ingredients: Gelatine, Citric Acid, Acidity Regulator: Trisodium Citrate, Flavourings, Sweeteners (Aspartame, Acesulfame K), Colours (Quinoline Yellow, Sunset Yellow FCF). **WARNING:** Contains a source of Phenylalanine. As defined by the FAC guidelines (when prepared as directed).
Produced under licence by Premier Ambient Products (UK) Limited.
® Registered trade mark of Société des Produits Nestlé S.A.

Topic 9 Study Guide 1 — Mechanical and Industrial Equipment

Here's what you need to know...

about how industrial processing equipment differs from domestic equipment.

See *Design & Make It! Food Technology* Revised pages 42–43, 50–51, 87 (34–35, 42–43, 79, 126 earlier edition).

KEYWORDS
Do you know what the following terms mean?
- Domestic
- Industrial

WWW.
Go to:
www.j-sainsbury.co.uk/education/tasteofsuccess/secondary.htm

Industrial Processing Equipment

Making a **batch** of food products in a factory is very different from making one at home. Although the basic processes are similar, the tools and equipment involved are not.

The most common processes in an industrial kitchen include:

- Mixing
- Cutting
- Forming (shaping)

Process	Domestic equipment	Industrial equipment
Mixing e.g. beating, whisking, kneading, stirring, rubbing in, creaming.	Fork, spoons, hand whisks, small hand held or table top food mixer, bowl size 3+ litres.	Large balloon whisks, rotary whisks, heavy-duty food processors, blenders and mixers. Large floor-standing bowl size 25+ litres, speed controls.
Cutting e.g. slicing, shredding, grating.	Knives, hand-held grater, pastry cutters, vegetable peelers, table top food processor.	Mandolins, large-scale food processors with wide variety of blades, speed controls, templates to control size and shape, electric food slicer.
Forming (shaping) e.g. piping, shaping pastries, coating.	Piping bag, fork, knife, dishes, rolling pins.	Large-scale moulds for shaping foods before they 'set' Piping bags with a variety of nozzles for decorative effects, preformed tins to shape products, rollers to maintain thickness and dimensions during preparation, burger presses, mincer.

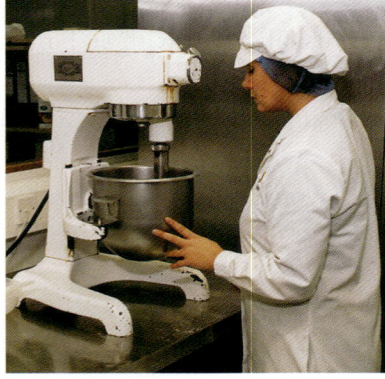

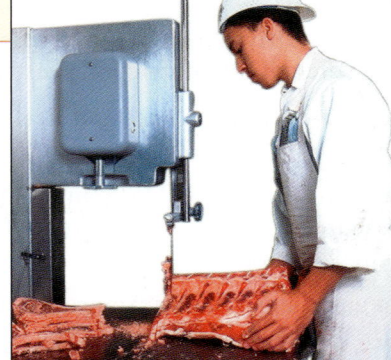

Written Question

Spend about 6 minutes answering the following question. You will need some paper and something to write with.

Complete the chart opposite to show how the choice of processing equipment may differ between domestic and industrial production of Cornish pasties. *(6 marks)*

Process	Domestic kitchen equipment choice	Industrial kitchen equipment choice
Preparing pastry		
Chopping vegetables		
Shaping pasty		

56

Topic 9 Study Guide 2 — Mechanical and Industrial Equipment

Here's what you need to know...

about how equipment may be used to aid consistency of outcome in food products.

See *Design & Make It! Food Technology* Revised pages 53, 59, 144–145 (45, 51, 136–137 earlier edition).

KEYWORDS
Do you know what the following term means?
- Consistency

Making It Consistently

Food production systems aim to produce high quality, **consistent** products, that is to say each product is made to the same standard.

Consistency is achieved by each product in every batch having the same:

- quantities of ingredients used
- amount of filling, coating, casing
- colour
- shape
- texture
- strength of flavour
- size
- **nutritional content**

Hand Made or Machine Made?

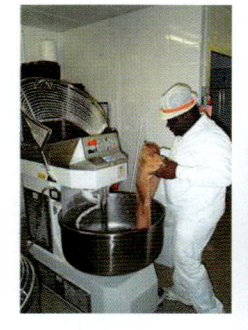

Human error means that hand produced food products are not as accurate and consistent as those made by machinery. **Automated** equipment can repeat tasks many times without getting tired or risking workers' **health and safety**.

Choosing the Right Equipment

The correct choice of equipment is essential to maintaining consistency during manufacture. When choosing equipment producers consider if the item to be used can provide:

- a range of attachments, cutters, templates or presses to give **standard dimensions** and shapes to foods.
- time settings to ensure all products are mixed or cooked for exactly the same time.
- speed settings so that all products are processed at the same time to ensure consistency of texture/rise.

Useful equipment may include food processors, blenders, mixers, electronic scales, coffee makers, pasta machines, mincers, electric slicers/peelers.

Written Question

Spend about 6 minutes answering the following question. You will need some paper and something to write with.

The three main components of a lemon meringue pie are pastry, lemon filling and meringue topping. Name two qualities of each of these that might be tested during manufacture to ensure all products are consistent. *(6 marks)*

Topic 9 Study Guide 3 — Mechanical and Industrial Equipment

Here's what you need to know...

about the different types of equipment that may be used for computer-controlled processes.

See *Design and Make It! Food Technology* Revised pages 42–43, 120–121, 135 (34–35, 112–113, 127 earlier edition).

KEYWORDS
Do you know what the following terms mean?
- Computer controlled
- Tunnel oven
- Combi oven
- Thermostatically controlled

WWW.
Go to:
www.foodtech.org.uk

Putting a Computer in Charge

Much of the large equipment used in industrial production can be **computer controlled**. Temperatures and timings may be controlled by computers. Many computers are also set up with alarms that alert workers should temperatures or times become faulty. Production problems can then be remedied before poor quality products pass through the production system.

Computer Controlled Industrial Production Equipment

- **Tunnel ovens**: products pass through an elongated oven that can be kept at a constant, monitored temperature.
- **Combi ovens**: usually controlled by a microprocessor, can be pre-programmed to give consistent products. These often have digital displays.
- Microwaves: higher **wattage** than domestic microwaves, so they cook more quickly. Some can be programmed and offer defrosting and browning functions.
- Deep fat fryers: **thermostatically controlled**. Computerised control of oil temperature and time of cooking.
- Chillers: to store foods safely before and after production.
- Ice cream makers: special cabinets kept at –17 °C
- Freezers: lower temperatures (–18 to –27 °C) than domestic freezers (–18 °C). **Blast freezers** will lower temperature of foods rapidly.
- Refrigerators: separate stainless steel refrigerators for raw and cooked foods. Built-in **sensors**, thermometers and automatic defrost make them different from a domestic refrigerator.

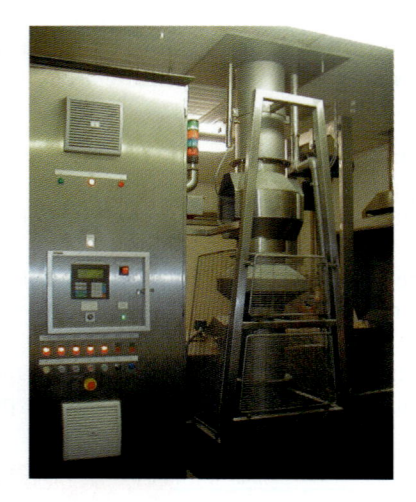

A computer controlled deep fat fryer.

Written Question

Spend about 4 minutes answering the following question. You will need some paper and something to write with.

A fish and chip shop wishes to install computer controlled food processing and storage equipment. Explain two opportunities where this small retail outlet might use this new equipment. *(4 marks)*

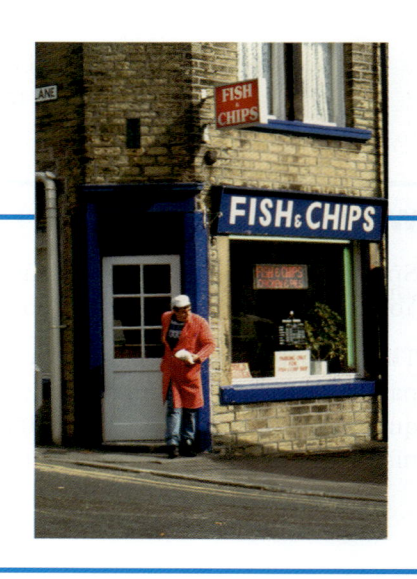

Topic 10 Study Guide 1 — Industrial Food Safety

Here's what you need to know...

about the role of micro-organisms and enzymes in the manufacture of food products.

See *Design & Make It! Food Technology* Revised pages 63, 64–65, 94–95 (55, 56–57, 86–87 earlier edition).

KEYWORDS
Do you know what the following terms mean?
- Microbiology
- Bacteria
- Yeast
- Moulds
- Micro-organisms
- Microbes
- Pathogens
- Enzymes

WWW.
Go to:
www.foodlink.org.uk/azlist.asp

Microbiology

Microbiology is the study of **bacteria**, **yeasts** and **moulds** – single-celled organisms that are known as **micro-organisms**. There are **harmful** micro-organisms and **helpful** micro-organisms. Some can cause food products to spoil and some micro-organisms can cause food poisoning. However, other micro-organisms can be used to enhance food products. Certain types of bacteria can be helpful in making yoghurt and blue cheeses, for example, and **Quorn** is manufactured by fermenting fungi.

Micro-organisms (sometimes called **microbes**) are living cells – they live, reproduce and die. They thrive in environments that provide moisture, warmth, enough time for growth and some form of food. Salt, an **alkali**, effectively prevents micro-organisms from growing. Extreme heat and high levels of **acidity** also prevent micro-organism growth.

Bacteria

Bacteria are found everywhere and most of them are completely harmless. However, some bacteria are responsible for causing food poisoning. This group of bacteria is called **pathogens**.

Pathogens can multiply very quickly in certain conditions. Not being able to see or smell pathogens makes them difficult to detect. They can be very dangerous and must be destroyed during food processing. Pathogens are destroyed by creating and controlling conditions that are not suitable for **bacterial growth**.

- Very high temperatures kill bacteria, and processes like **pasteurisation** have been developed to do this during food processing.
- Bacteria need moisture: so drying out or freezing food can prevent growth.
- Bacteria also don't like very sugary or very salty conditions.

Food manufacturers do all they can to prevent **contamination** during food processing.

Yeasts

Yeasts grow on foods that contain sugar. They help to **ferment** fruits to make alcohol and act as **raising agents** in breads. However, over time they can also harm fruits and jam products.

Moulds

Moulds may look unpleasant, but they are not pathogens. They particularly grow on bread, fruit, meat and cheese. Harmless moulds are used to create products such as Stilton cheese.

Enzymes

An **enzyme** is a protein that acts as a **catalyst**. It breaks down tissue in meat or cell walls in fruit, causing meat to tenderise and fruit to ripen. Enzymes can be used to artificially speed up a ripening stage.

Enzymes may also need to be controlled. For example, **enzymic browning** is the process that makes cut slices of fruit turn brown when they are exposed to the air. It can be controlled by stopping contact with the air (putting the slices under water), using acids (such as lemon juice), or boiling.

Written Question

Spend about 9 minutes answering the following question. You will need some paper and something to write with.

i) Briefly state what pathogens are and explain why they are of particular concern to the food industry. *(5 marks)*

ii) Explain how some micro-organisms can be used to produce safe foods. *(4 marks)*

59

Topic 10 Study Guide 2 | Industrial Food Safety

Here's what you need to know...

about the risks of spoilage due to food contamination.

See *Design & Make It! Food Technology* Revised pages 64–65 (56–57 earlier edition).

KEYWORDS
Do you know what the following terms mean?
- Contamination
- Spoilage
- Rancidity
- Mould free shelf-life

Contamination and Spoilage

Steps need to be taken at all stages of food supply to prevent **contamination** and **spoilage** and to avoid **wastage**. These steps include correct harvesting, transport, storage, packaging and safety and hygiene procedures. These are discussed in more detail in Sections 4 and 5 of this topic.

What is Food Contamination?

Food contamination happens when potentially harmful substances get into food products. This is usually accidental, but (very rarely) people deliberately contaminate products to cause harm. **Tamperproof packaging** is designed to expose deliberate contamination.

Contaminants can be chemical, biological or physical. For example:

- **chemical** – the use of chemical cleaners in food areas, or pesticides and fertilisers.
- **biological** – cross-contamination of bacteria between foods, mould growth, insects on fruit, viral infection, etc.
- **physical** – bits of metals, grit, waste matter in foods.

Contaminants can affect the safety of foods and the quality of foods.

What is Spoilage?

Food naturally changes over time. For example, you might wait a couple of days after buying a melon for it to ripen. If you leave it too long, it will start to decay. Spoilage happens in between ripening and decaying.

Bruising, wilting, shrivelling, mould growth, or discolouration, are signs of spoilage in fruits and vegetables. These happen naturally over time, but they may also be due to the effects of drought or frost on vegetables and fruits.

Rancidity

Rancidity is **spoilage** of fatty products, like peanuts, crisps and snack foods. Rancidity causes 'off' smells and flavours. Packaging is often adapted to prevent rancidity by **modifying** (changing) the atmosphere in the pack to slow down this natural process. This kind of packaging is called **Modified Atmosphere Packaging (MAP)**.

Mould

Spoilage can occur at any time. Spoilage of many food products is due to moulds. Signs of mould are easily seen on products such as bread or cakes.

Manufacturers need their products to be on the shelves for as long as possible before they have to be discarded, to make sure they can get maximum sales. They know that customers will not buy mouldy food. So the **mould free shelf-life** of a packaged food product is very important to the manufacturer and retailer. It is the time a product can be assured to be mould free in **ambient storage**.

Written Question

Spend about 8 minutes answering the following question. You will need some paper and something to write with.

The food industry needs to apply appropriate safe food handling techniques in order to supply attractive and acceptable products.

i) In the supply process of vegetables, give two examples where handling techniques could affect the quality of the products.

(2 marks)

ii) Explain how handling techniques for a food product or products could result in contamination and spoilage. What would be the consequences of this for the consumer?

(6 marks)

Topic 10 Study Guide 3 — Industrial Food Safety

Here's what you need to know...

about risk assessment.

See *Design & Make It! Food Technology* Revised pages 134–137 (126–129 earlier edition).

KEYWORDS
Do you know what the following terms mean?
- Risk assessment
- HACCP

WWW.
Go to:
www.chilledfood.org
(Click on Information for Students)

Taking the Risk

Problems in food processing can have serious consequences. For example, **contamination** of a food product could lead to **food poisoning**. Problems that could cause harm to a consumer are called **hazards**.

There is an important difference between a hazard and a **risk**. A risk tells you how likely it is that a problem will happen. A hazard is the problem itself. If something is risky, we know it means there's likely to be a hazard involved.

Risk assessment helps to make food operations safe by minimising the risk of hazards. Risk assessment is about identifying what hazards might happen, how likely they are to happen, and what the result would be if they did happen. Risk assessment calculates where the risks of hazards are in a process, and how to make things as safe as possible.

Assessing risks in the food business is very important. Apart from the immediate health risk to the consumer, bad publicity from food poisoning could result in **product recall**, production being stopped and expensive fines.

What are the Hazards?

The identification of hazards is the key to risk analysis and assessment. There are three main types of hazard in food production:

- **biological** hazards – bacterial **contamination**, mould growth, etc.
- **chemical** hazards – contamination from chemicals, such as pesticides or cleaning fluids.
- **physical** – contamination from physical objects, such as waste material, bits of machinery, hairnets, etc.

Risk assessment in food production looks particularly at:

- timings – for example, undercooking or overcooking.
- temperature – temperatures not being high or low enough.
- ingredients – for example, the risk of **spoilage** of raw materials.
- processing methods – for example, the physical or chemical **contamination** hazards in the process.
- packaging – **labelling** details for re-heating, user instructions and **date marks**.

If risk assessment shows that hazards are likely to occur, changes will have to be made to reduce the risks. If there are too many risks it is possible that the food product will have to be redesigned.

Written Question

Spend about 12 minutes answering the following question. You will need some paper and something to write with.

i) Identify four examples of where risks can occur during the manufacturing of food. Explain what the risks might be. *(8 marks)*

ii) Give four examples of the potential causes of such risks. *(4 marks)*

The Risk Assessment Process

Each stage and step of processing is carefully considered during prototype testing. A **HACCP** (Hazard Analysis and Critical Control Points) is drawn up to put controls into place to reduce risks during large-scale production.

During production the control points are carefully **monitored** to provide evidence that hazards are being eliminated. In most cases, **ICT** is used for data collection and logging.

An effective risk assessment system should result in a bacteria-free, wrapped and packed food product delivered to retail outlets in conditions that are unsuitable for **micro-organisms** to grow in.

Topic 10 Study Guide 4 — Industrial Food Safety

Here's what you need to know...

about safety and hygiene rules in food manufacturing.

See *Design & Make It! Food Technology* Revised pages 62–65 (54–57 earlier edition).

KEYWORDS

Do you know what the following terms mean?
- Hygiene
- Low-risk foods
- Medium-risk food
- High-risk foods
- Cross-contamination

Hygiene at Work

The safety of each new food product is carefully planned to minimise the risks of **contamination** during stages in production, packaging and distribution. It is very important for food safety that everyone involved in the process makes sure **hygiene** standards never drop.

Safety and hygiene are very important for all those who handle food directly during production. Manufacturers have specific guidelines about how food handlers work, what they wear, and what they know.

Food hygiene — Wash only hands here

High, Medium and Low-risk Food Products

Not all food products carry the same risk of biological contamination.

- **Low-risk foods** are those with high acid or sugar content, raw vegetables, edible oils and fats.
- **Medium-risk foods** include dried or frozen products, freshly processed products and those with a high fat content.
- **High-risk foods** include unprocessed meat, fish and eggs and dairy products.

High and Low-risk Areas of Food Manufacture

In a factory, low-risk areas are the areas where ingredients arrive and ingredients are prepared. Cooking will follow this and the high temperatures will destroy any harmful bacteria. After processing, during sealing and packing, food products are in the high-risk area of a factory. This is because any contamination at this point will remain in the product until it is purchased and then used.

Cross-contamination

During production and storage **micro-organisms** can easily pass from raw to cooked foods. This can cause infection. It is therefore essential to avoid the danger of **cross-contamination**. This involves taking steps to ensure that:

- raw and cooked foods are kept separate.
- juices from raw foods do not drip on to cooked foods in storage.
- bacteria are not spread between hands, work-surfaces and equipment.

Legislation

Food safety and food hygiene are strictly regulated by the law and industry codes of practice. The **Food Safety Act (1995)** sets out the law for manufacturers in the European Union. The **Health and Safety Executive (HSE)** makes sure safety rules and regulations are obeyed so that food production remains safe.

Environmental Health Officers work in their local area to make sure that factories and retail outlets obey the Food Safety Act and carry out proper food hygiene procedures.

Making sure new products will be produced safely and hygienically is a major aspect of the development of manufacturing specifications in test kitchens. Manufacturers also need to give the right advice to consumers about handling and preparing their products in the home.

Written Question

Spend about 10 minutes answering the following question. You will need some paper and something to write with.

Food safety is very important to manufacturers, and risk assessment is used to identify hazards and minimise the risk of them occurring.

For each of the stages in the production process shown in the chart below, identify one hazard that might occur and describe how the risk of this hazard could be minimised. *(10 marks)*

Storage	Hazard	Risk minimised by:
i) Storage of raw materials	Cross-contamination	Raw and cooked ingredients should be stored separately.
ii) Preparation of ingredients	Biological contamination from food handlers having bacteria on hands	All food handlers having to wash hands with anti-bacterial soap before handling food
iii) Cooking of ingredients	Bacteria still alive after cooking, like listeria or E-coli bacteria	Cooking thoroughly so that the bacteria are all killed off and do not cause food poisoning
iv) Packaging	Physical contamination	Packaging happening in high risk area, regular checks
v) Transporting	Products squashed when stacked	Making sure packaging is strong enough for transport

Topic 10 Study Guide 5 — Industrial Food Safety

Here's what you need to know...

about food preservation and storage.

See *Design & Make It! Food Technology* Revised pages 96–99 (88–91 earlier edition).

KEYWORDS
Do you know what the following terms mean?
- Storage
- High temperature preservation
- Low temperature preservation
- Chemical preservation
- Drying
- Non-perishable foods
- Perishable foods
- Modified Atmosphere Packaging (MAP)

WWW.
Go to:
www.nutrition.org.uk

Preservation

Different food products need different methods of storage to help maintain their quality over time, and to avoid the risk of bacterial **contamination**. The method of storage used also often depends on the preparation and **preservation** processes used during manufacture. During preparation, food products can be preserved by:

Using high temperatures
High temperature methods include canning, UHT (ultra-heat treatment), **sterilisation** and **pasteurisation**. Many products are canned. Canning involves intense heat treatment. Although it provides an extremely long shelf-life, these very high temperatures affect the quality of the flavour, texture and **nutritional value** of the product.

Using low temperatures
Low temperature methods involve chilling or freezing. Chilling extends the shelf-life of the product by a number of days, and maintains the quality of the product very well.

Freezing, if carried out quickly, causes small ice crystals to form in the food that do very little damage to the food structure. Freezing gives lengthy storage times for products. After thawing, the food generally has excellent quality: it has usually kept its original flavour, texture, colour and nutritional profile. Exceptions to this include bananas and whole eggs, which do not freeze, and products such as tomatoes, which freeze but become mushy on thawing.

Using chemicals
Salt can be used to preserve meat, fish and vegetables and adds flavour at the same time. Vinegar is acidic, and therefore prevents bacterial growth. High concentrations of sugar also act as a preservative. Some products, such as chutneys, use a combination of salt, vinegar and sugar.

Removing moisture
Micro-organisms cannot develop without moisture, so **drying** is a useful method for certain products such as fruit and vegetables, coffee, potatoes, etc. There is a range of industrial techniques available, such as hot air drying, spray drying and roller drying. **Accelerated Freeze Drying (AFD)** provides improved colour and flavour.

When rehydrated there is often a significant change to the colour, texture, flavour, and nutritional value of the original food product.

Storage Environment

After preparation, food usually requires storage by the manufacturer, the retailer and, finally, the consumer. It is extremely important for the quality of food components that they are stored correctly and appropriately. In industry, sophisticated systems are used to control the storage of foods, such as **stock rotation** and **temperature control**.

Storage Times

The storage time for a food product relates to the safety of the food. Some food products can be stored at **ambient temperature** or **shelf temperature** in a shop. These types of foods are known as **non-perishables**. The length of time they can remain on display is indicated by a '**best before**' date. If consumed later than that they would be safe but may have poor quality in texture, flavour or colour.

Perishable foods are presented with '**display until**' and '**use by**' dates. After the use by date perishable food must be thrown away. In some cases the storage time relates to the quality of the food – mature cheeses develop better, stronger flavours, as do some meats.

Modified Atmosphere Packaging (MAP)

Some products, such as crisps and salads, can be placed inside packages that contain gases that help prevent the product going off. These retain the quality of the product very well.

Written Question

Spend about 12 minutes answering the following question. You will need some paper and something to write with.

Removing moisture (drying) is a common method of preserving food products.

i) Name three other conditions that can be changed in order to preserve vegetables, lasagne and fruits. *(3 marks)*

ii) Explain how and why these changes have an effect on the quality of the products. *(9 marks)*

63